Early Acclaim for
UNEXPECTED LEADER

"Great read! There are indeed unexpected leaders among us. They show up daily in various industries and help many by sharing their wisdom. I enjoyed reading the team collaboration of each author's vision on what attributes they felt defines leadership. The positive take away as a reader, although each Author's perspective is uniquely defined by their industry knowledge, ALL shared a common obvious thread of passion in their respective fields to help empower others. Hence good leaders come from people who have a passion for the field of work they are in."

—Shawn Remillard, Former Global Director for UPS

"I am certified in VUCA leadership which stands for Volatility, Uncertainty, Complexity, and Ambiguity. The United States Military teaches the principles of VUCA to help their officers and enlisted servicemen and women to overcome challenges on the battlefield and in civilian life. The different perspectives on leadership outlined in this book embody the spirit of VUCA from how to take ownership of your personal health to how to develop various leadership skills to lead a team and much more. The steps outlined in the book are easy to follow and can be implemented by anyone in any stage of their life. I highly recommend read as these principles are effective and easily implemented!"

—Sanjay Raja, Author/ Speaker/ Media Personality/ Host of The *Food Talk* TV Show

"What I like most about Unexpected Leader is the collection of perspectives from so many industry experts from countries all over the world. There is resounding proof in the book that supports the theory that in order to lead others, you must learn to lead yourself first. The tools and strategies are broken down in a way that is easy to understand and apply. I can't wait to utilize the teachings with my own team!"

—Tinsley English, Insurance Operations, Keynote Speaker and Bestselling Author of *Grit Growth & Gumption*

"I loved the common thread amongst the co-authors, emphasizing that a true leader begins with the self. The development of qualities of integrity, to motivate and inspire others, all originates from the journey of finding authenticity within. Just as a leader starts with self, an organization thrives when each part is in harmony, reflecting the importance of authenticity and self-connection in leadership."

—Satie Narain-Simon, CPA Former tax auditor, former VP of Toronto TSO Audit, Finance, Science (AFS), co-author, international motivational speaker

"Without vision, you cannot lead yourself or others. Vision is the key to leadership, but as evidenced by the many amazing authors, you must uncover what stands in the way of your vision. Unexpected Leader offers a diverse look at leadership covering multiple industries but provides many useful resources to help leaders in any industry unlock what stands in the way of your authentic leadership blossoming."

—Kathleen Kennedy, APR President and Founder, Center for Communication and Engagement Veteran education communication and leadership expert

UNEXPECTED LEADER

11 TOOLS FOR
TRANSFORMATIONAL
LEADERSHIP

Melanie Warner/ Dr. Hélène Bertrand

Chanie Twersky/ Sandy Sandler/ Jenny Ferguson

Nigel Smart/ Angela Dingle/ Dr. Kristina Wachter

Laura Davis/ Mia Reed/ Samantha Taylor

Defining Moments Press

Cover Design: 99designs
Editing: Dona Watson
Formatting: Kat Spencer

ISBN#: 979-8-9901587-0-2 (ebook)

ISBN#: 979-8-9901587-1-9 (print)

PRESS

Want More Direction from Defining Moments Press?

At Defining Moments Press, we represent authors, speakers and business owners who are subject-matter experts. With over 300 different industry-specific specialists, our goal is to help you succeed in both personal and professional growth.

**Hire one of our certified speakers to
speak at your next event.**

**Hire one of our experts for
private or group training.**

**HIRE AN EXPERT AT:
www.mydefiningmoments.com**

DEDICATION

I would like to dedicate this book to my dad, John Warner, who has always led by example.

And to my mom, Judy Warner, who has always led our family with love, respect and kindness.

Together, they taught me about teamwork, business, marriage, contribution, humor and leadership—both in and out of the office.

I would also like to dedicate this to all leaders including the unexpected ones and those yet to step into leadership.

—Melanie Warner

TABLE OF CONTENTS

ACKNOWLEDGEMENTS

I would like to thank each of the co-authors who helped make this project possible. You are all such amazing leaders and I am honored to take this book journey with you.

Thank you to our incredible team who helped put this book together: Amber Torres, Kat Spencer, Shiran Cohen, Micah Requita, Jasmin Marcos, Antigone Klima, Michael Santiago, Shannon Dean, Erin-Kate Whitcomb, Ligia Montani and Dona Watson.

Thank you to my kids, Kyla, Cole & Hudson Kennedy for making a mother out of me and believing in my leadership when it was still experimental. I feel I owe you therapy for life after all of the life-coaching experiments I put you through.

Thank you to my hero, Shawn Remillard, for the countless hours of brainstorming, mind-mapping, gallons of coffee, buckets of wine (and whine), witnessing my meltdowns, positivity, patience, laughter, breakfast in bed, unofficial consulting, and unwavering support.

—Melanie Warner

INTRODUCTION

Unlock the secrets of leadership and elevate your performance with *Unexpected Leader: 11 Tools for Transformational Leadership*. This book is your essential companion on the journey to becoming a stronger leader, manager and trainer, fostering leadership skills that transcend all aspects of life and business.

Only 10% of people are born as leaders. So, the majority of leaders were developed. And most will tell you they didn't see themselves as leaders.

In a world where leadership is the most valuable and profitable skill often overlooked, this book emerges as a beacon for those seeking to inspire and guide others. Whether you lead a work team, a sports team, a family, a nonprofit, or all of the above, *Unexpected Leader* equips you with the strategies that will set you apart.

For those new to leadership, dive into 11 insightful chapters, each brimming with actionable tools, strategies and inspirational stories. Implement these immediately with your team members or clients to kick-start your leadership journey.

Seasoned leaders, fear not! *Unexpected Leader* offers a plethora of perspectives around leadership that will complement your existing techniques. Each chapter unveils high-level leadership strategies and philosophies, accompanied by practical activities and tools requiring minimal preparation.

This book stands out by showcasing wisdom from elite coaches, mentors, psychologists, doctors, business owners, and lifestyle experts worldwide. These experts, hailing from the United States, Canada, and Europe, bring diverse insights that supplement your knowledge as a life coach.

1

The co-authors, a distinguished group trained by luminaries such as Tony Robbins, John Maxwell, Napoleon Hill, Dr. Wayne Dyer and more, share their wealth of experience and life lessons on leadership. From communication experts and senior business executives to TEDx speakers and former pro athletes, this dynamic group covers it all.

Meet the exceptional co-authors: Melanie Warner, Dr. Hélène Bertrand, Chanie Twersky, Sandy Sandler, Jenny Ferguson, Nigel Smart, Angela Dingle, Dr. Kristina Wachter, Laura Davis, Mia Reed, and Samantha Taylor. Together, they bring a fusion of expertise that promises to transform both leaders and their teams.

Unexpected Leader is not just a book—it's a roadmap to success in different coaching situations. Let these leaders guide you on a transformative journey, applying universal principles to multiple facets of life and business. Embrace the unexpected and emerge as the leader you were meant to be.

CHAPTER ONE

Defining Moments in Leadership
By Melanie Warner

What is leadership? Myles Munroe said it this way: "Leadership is the capacity to influence others through inspiration, motivated by passion, generated by vision, produced by conviction, ignited by purpose."

Mark Twain said the following: "There are two important days of your life. One is the day you are born and the other is the day when you discover WHY you were born."

I like to say when purpose and leadership come together, that is a "defining moment."

A defining moment can happen in a company. A defining moment can happen in a relationship. A defining moment can happen in a health diagnosis. And defining moments can happen when one person reaches out to be kind to another.

My defining moment was August 31, 2005. I was in a hospital after an accident. I had no idea that I was running out of blood and 90 seconds away from dying. A doctor came in and said, "You might not make it." I thought, "What about my family? What about my unfinished book? What about my laundry?"

I thought of all the unfinished things in my life. "*I can't die! I have too much to do.*" Luckily, I had a blood transfusion and it saved my life.

Two days later, I had another defining moment. I held my son, Carson, as he took his last breath.

Nothing prepared me for that moment. I didn't know how to deal with my grief. I shut down. That began a long journey of loss.

I shut down my entire business that I had spent 20 years building. It was my only source of income. I got divorced after 16 years of marriage. I went through bankruptcy, foreclosure, and tax audits. I even had to defend myself in federal tax court because I couldn't afford to hire anyone else.

I felt like I had it all and lost it all. I went from hero to zero. From Prada to nada—almost overnight. I had $3.6 million in debt. I feared that it would take me another 20 years to build another business and dig myself out of that hole. I was a single mom with three kids. I had no time to waste; I had to figure something out … quickly.

I became the unexpected leader in my own life first, then for my family. None of us knows what we can do until we have to.

In 18 months, I was able to rebuild my entire life to $4 million dollars with a new business. I thought at the time that it was all a setback. I didn't realize that all of the lessons I learned in that journey were to set me up for the success I currently have in my life. I thought I was being buried … but I was being planted—for the life I have today.

Are Leaders Born or Developed?

According to a Gallup survey, only one in 10 people actually possess the talent to manage or lead people.

I never saw myself as a leader. I thought if I was just the boss, that would make me a good leader. At some point in our lives, we all experience leadership. It can be either really great leadership or really crappy leadership. Although it's challenging to articulate, the impact is profound. Whether it's a boss, teacher, parent, or coach, a great leader leaves a lasting impression and we are happier, more engaged and perform better as a result of their guidance.

But none of us are born knowing how to be a leader, even if we possess that rare quality. In a world where true leadership and a clear sense of purpose often seem elusive, it's essential to remember that the responsibility lies with all of us. True leadership is not just about those in positions of power; it's about each one of us taking the initiative to lead by example, inspire others, and foster a sense of purpose within ourselves and our communities. By recognizing our individual roles in shaping the world and actively seeking our purpose, we can collectively create a brighter and more purposeful future for all.

Purpose Exercise™

Once you learn the Purpose Exercise, you'll never forget it. Your life will never be the same again. The most important thing for you to get what you want, is the ability to know exactly what you were put on this planet to do.

I am going to share with you a special tool that I have shared all over the world with millions of people in the last 15 years. I've done it on planes, trains and automobiles. Recently, I did this at an event in India with 700,000 people!

This was the most powerful thing that helped me get my life back on track. It only takes a few minutes.

I'm going to ask you three QUESTIONS that you probably have never asked yourself before. I can also tell you that no two people have EVER answered these three questions in the exact same way.

Find a quiet place without distractions. Turn off your phone. Grab a sheet of paper. Take a deep breath. Here we go!

The first question is:

1. *What are you really good at that comes naturally to you, but is difficult for other people?*

Don't overthink this. Just jot down the first thing that comes to mind.

The next question is:

> 2. *What would you do for free the next two or three years if you could do anything you wanted to do and didn't have to worry about money?*

If all of your bills were paid, what would you do?

Now for the final question:

> 3. *What do you do to give back—to people or the planet?*

Maybe you donate time, talent or treasure. Maybe you recycle. Think about one key thing you do to give back.

Now look at all of your answers. Do you have a different answer for each question? Or are they all the same?

If all of the answers are the same, then THAT THING IS YOUR PURPOSE. If they are different, then make an adjustment in your life or business until they align. It really is that simple.

Now look at your fingertips. Try to find someone else with the same fingerprint ... it's impossible.

Your purpose is as unique as your fingerprint. And that is EXACTLY how you have an individual purpose that serves as a vital role in your life and in your career or your business.

If you are the owner of a company, you often fear that if people find their true purpose they might leave. It's quite the opposite. According to a recent article from Forbes, employee engagement and wellness are taking precedence in the business world. This is not an HR responsibility and yet 87% of employees expect their employer to support their work/life balance. Employees must feel that they are operating within their purpose to feel connected and engaged.

If you are an employee, then purpose is critical to connection, performance and retention to stay at a company.

Think of your company as a human body. Perhaps this is why a business is called an ORGANization. Each role in a company is just as important as each organ is to a human body.

You might think because you are "just a receptionist" that you are the low man or woman on the totem pole. You might feel like a cog in the wheel. But just like a kidney, you are filtering all things incoming and processing them to send to other vital organs for healthy function. It's actually one of the most important roles as this is often the first contact a potential customer has with the company.

Your founder might be the heart and soul of the company.

What are the salespeople? They are the legs of the company, the mouth and the guts. Sometimes, they are the liver (in more social roles). Nothing happens in a company without sales.

Marketing is the voice of the company.

Your CEO might just be the face.

Your CFO might be the brains of your company—or the wallet.

Your clients are the food, lifeblood or circulation.

Your HR department is the nervous system that sends warning signals to other organs.

Your managers are the muscles that hold everything together. When they are strained, nothing seems to function well and the pain can be sharp.

Every single one of you has a purpose.

Now I know some of you are wondering who represents the "nether regions" of your company? You know ... the crotch.

It could be your boss. It could be a client. Or could even be YOU!

Think about this ... who is in therapy because of you? Who wants to quit today because of you?

Have you ever had someone come to you and ask for advice and then they do the exact opposite of what you told them to do? I lovingly call those people *askholes*.

And what about the difficult ones who don't listen, undermine every system or policy, challenge your authority, are outspoken or have power issues? They slowly chip away at your culture and vision.

Just like cancer, negativity and bad juju can spread quickly throughout the entire body or organization. If you don't remove it, then it ends all function for the rest of the organs.

We now live in a global village where everyone is striving for more. We need leaders. We need more purposeful defining moments. When you strive to reach a dream, you are honoring the people you love.

My favorite thing to do is executive retreats. This is where we extract the blocks that are creating a kink in your hose to get life-giving water to your garden. It's leadership training on steroids. Maybe you need an ayahuasca trip. Maybe you need your own healing. Maybe you need to be a better leader. Maybe your team is missing a critical piece. Maybe you just need to hang with other winners.

Melanie Warner is one of the top transformational leadership experts in the world. Melanie is an international keynote speaker, a USA Today and Wall Street Journal Bestselling author and CEO of Defining Moments Press. She has coached thousands of people on finding their purpose and monetizing their knowledge through leadership. Melanie has owned magazines and newspapers for over 30 years. She is also a journalist and has been featured or written for Entrepreneur, Fortune, Forbes, CNN, the Rolling Stone and is the Executive Producer of the TV show, The Food Talk, airing in 250 million homes. She has also been hired and endorsed by Tony Robbins, Dean Graziosi and the founders of Chicken Soup for the Soul, Mark Victor Hansen & Jack Canfield. She has worked with companies, government organizations, C-suite executives, celebrities, athletes, authors, speakers and coaches to harness and leverage the power of purpose to create the next generation of leaders.

To book Melanie as a speaker or for more information about her transformational leadership training, please contact her via email.

Email: Melanie@mydefiningmoments.com
Website: www.mydefiningmoments.com
LinkedIn:https://www.linkedin.com/in/melanie-warner-defining-moments

CHAPTER TWO

Empowering Yourself to Relieve Low Back Pain
By Dr. Hélène Bertrand

As a physician with 55 years of experience in family medicine, my lifelong mission has been to liberate people from the shackles of pain without resorting to surgery or medications. In this chapter, I'm excited to share with you a powerful tool that can help you eliminate your own low back pain in just two minutes.

The Quest for Pain Relief

How many of you have experienced the torment of low back pain? Or perhaps you know someone close to you who has suffered from this debilitating condition? It's a widespread issue that plagues billions of individuals worldwide. The human body possesses an incredible capacity to heal itself, and if your pain resulted from an injury, it should have healed by now, shouldn't it? So, what is causing this persistent pain?

Unraveling the Mystery

My journey led me to a groundbreaking discovery: a way to examine the back that reveals precisely where the pain originates. Let's embark on this exploration together. Please stand up and place your fingers firmly into your buttocks, about two to three inches on either side of the middle, starting at the level of the tailbone. While maintaining this pressure, move your fingers upwards until you encounter a bony obstruction on either side. If pressing below one of these bony obstacles causes discomfort, you have identified the joint responsible for your pain. Ask a friend or check in the mirror to see if one of your fingers is higher than the other and, if so, which one.

If the finger on the painful side is either higher or lower than the other, it indicates that the joint is displaced. So, what is this joint we've just pinpointed? It's the one that connects your sacrum, the triangular bone at the base of your spine, to your pelvic bones—the sacroiliac (SI) joint. Your pelvic bones are easy to locate; you're sitting on them right now.

Understanding the Significance of Pelvic Bones

Let's delve deeper into the anatomy of your pelvic bones. Place your hands on either side of your body and begin at the waist. Push downward to feel the top of your pelvic bones, known as the iliac crest. You can trace the iliac crest to the front, where it ends in a small bony point, and to the back, where you previously encountered it with your fingers. The bony protrusions you felt just above the SI joints during your self-examination were the extensions of the iliac crests on your back.

The Weight of Low Back Pain

Have you ever experienced excruciating low back pain that left you unable to walk, get out of bed, or perform your daily tasks? Even if you managed to carry on with these activities to some extent, did the pain still severely disrupt your life, affecting your sleep, work, family responsibilities, relationships, and even your sex life?

My guiding principle has always been clear: if you have a problem, find its root cause so you can solve it. In medicine, understanding the cause often leads to a straightforward treatment plan. When it comes to body pain, comprehending the underlying anatomy is the key to resolving it. For nerve-related pains, it's crucial to understand the nerves, their locations, the body areas they supply and the methods to calm them down.

The Revelation: Displaced Pelvic Bones

After 37 years of relentless research, I made a startling discovery: the primary cause of most low back pain lies in the displacement of pelvic bones. My personal journey towards relief began in 2003 when I attended a continuing education lecture with Dr. Murray Allen, a sports medicine specialist. I vividly remember saying to him, "My sacroiliac joints are killing me!" To my astonishment, he replied, "Come and see me, and I'll perform prolotherapy on you." My immediate reaction was, "Prolo what?" I was puzzled.

Dr. Allen went on to explain that the ligaments holding joints together have limited blood supply, making it challenging for them to heal naturally. Prolotherapy injects an irritant where the ligaments attach on the blood vessel–rich covering of the bone to produce inflammation, which starts the growth of new blood vessels within these ligaments. These are the roads the repair cells take to reinforce them with collagen, the building blocks of the human body. My personal experience with prolotherapy was transformative. Three treatments to my SI joints, one month apart, provided me with a year of pain-free living. Dr. Allen taught me the art of prolotherapy, enabling me to offer this relief to my patients. They were immensely grateful.

The Significance of the SI Joint

Now, you might be wondering why the SI joint plays such a critical role in low back pain. The answer lies in the sheer weight it bears. Unlike most animals, we humans are upright beings. Our entire upper body, including the head, arms, vital organs, and even our body fat, exerts continuous downward and outward pressure on the pelvic bones. This pressure tends to push the pelvic bones away from the sacrum, stressing the SI joints.

Moreover, our hip joints are nestled within the pelvic bones, subjecting the SI joints to additional jolts and shocks every time we take a step. These SI joints, unlike all the others that are smooth, are filled with bumps and hollows designed to absorb the shock from each footfall. However, their irregularities render them invisible to medical imaging techniques such as x-rays, CT scans, or MRIs, making SI joint pain frustratingly elusive for physicians. Ninety percent of all low back pain is labeled "nonspecific" as it cannot be diagnosed with conventional tests or medical imaging. Most of this pain comes from the SI joints.

The Role of Ligaments and Nerves

Understanding the source of SI joint pain involves recognizing the critical role of ligaments. Ligaments are bands of collagen that hold joints together, equipped with nerve endings that relay information to the brain about joint movements. Ligaments communicate the sensation of each movement—even the slightest shift.

Imagine closing your eyes and moving your fingers; you would instantly know the position of each finger. This sensory information is transmitted through nerves inside the ligaments surrounding your finger joints. When joints are out of place, the ligaments are stretched beyond their normal limits, causing the overstretched nerves within them to send pain signals to the brain. This pain serves as a warning sign, urging you to cease any actions that may further damage the joint.

Given this insight, consider the use of painkillers when dealing with joint pain. Painkillers merely mask the symptoms, offering temporary relief, while the underlying problem persists. Isn't it wiser to address the root cause?

A Lifelong Dedication to Pain Relief

In my final years of medical practice, I dedicated my focus to providing relief for individuals suffering from pain. I received referrals from other physicians for cases they deemed "hopeless," and astonishingly, 80% of these patients eventually found freedom from pain. My approach was simple yet powerful—identify the cause of the pain and develop techniques to address that cause, rather than relying on medications to mask the symptoms.

As I neared retirement after 55 years of practicing medicine, my original plan was to step away from the field. However, I found it impossible to rest when I knew that so many people were suffering, often misdiagnosed and offered limited options for pain relief, primarily surgery or addictive medications. Various other professions provided alternative treatments, such as chiropractic manipulation, physiotherapy, massage, or acupuncture, but still, the pain persisted.

A Turning Point

In 2011, I attended a conference where Dr. John Lyftogt from New Zealand introduced the concept of injecting dextrose (sugar water) around nerves that transmit pain signals to the brain. This approach intrigued me, and I began experimenting with it. To my astonishment, I witnessed immediate and complete relief from pain in my patients.

However, there was a challenge. Many of my patients suffered from diabetic neuropathic pain, and sugar is known to damage nerves in diabetic individuals. I needed an alternative. This quest led me to the discovery that injecting mannitol, a natural sweetener, around affected nerves could also bring rapid and complete pain relief.

The Birth of QR Cream

Observing the remarkable efficacy of mannitol, I collaborated with Marylene Kyriazis, a pharmacist. Together, we transformed this treatment into a cream. After extensive experimentation, we found a base cream that allowed mannitol to penetrate the skin effectively and reach irritated nerves. We named it QR Cream and our journey took a new direction.

We conducted research, distributing QR Cream to 235 individuals suffering from 289 types of pain, ranging from headaches to foot pain. The results were astounding, with an average pain relief of 53%. To put this into perspective, narcotics typically provide 36% relief, and anti-inflammatory medications offer an average of 23%. QR Cream was changing lives.

Empowering Self-Care

My mission expanded beyond clinical practice. I discovered numerous techniques that individuals could use at home to manage their pain, including changes in posture, specific exercises, recommended products, and even do-it-yourself orthotics using Kleenex and duct tape.

With Marylene, I established MaryHelene Enterprises Inc., offering QR Cream to the public. Our website, QRcream.com, provides a wealth of information on how to use QR Cream for different types of pain and offers guidance on other methods to find relief.

The Path Forward

I am not here by design, but by necessity. My initial plan was retirement, but I could not rest knowing that so many people were in pain, often misdiagnosed and offered limited solutions. My desire to bring relief to those who suffer has led to the creation of my book, *Low Back Pain: 3 Steps to Relief in 2 Minutes*. It provides comprehensive information on diagnosing the source of the pain and the two-minute exercise that can give immediate relief to over 80% of those who suffer from this condition.

I am also available as a keynote speaker, eager to educate groups of people on natural, non-surgical, and non-chemical ways to alleviate pain. My greatest joy is seeing individuals empowered to take control of their pain and find relief.

Conclusion

In this chapter, I've shared my journey of discovery and empowerment when it comes to relieving low back and other pain. From the identification of the SI joint as a common source of pain to the development of QR Cream, my mission has always been clear: to free individuals from the clutches of pain and provide them with the knowledge and tools to do the same for themselves.

By understanding the anatomy behind your pain, you can take the first step towards relief. Remember, pain is not a life sentence; it's a signal that something needs attention. With the right knowledge and tools, you can reclaim your life from the grips of pain and enjoy a future free from its burden.

I also have a corporate wellness program available so you can keep your morale high and employee sick days lower.

Dr. Hélène Bertrand taught, conducted research, and practiced family medicine for 55 years. In the last 20 years of her practice, she focused on finding ways to relieve pain. She wanted her patients to have access to techniques they could use to relieve their own pain. Among those, a new examination and treatment for low back pain that requires only a two-minute corrective exercise and has a 90% success rate in relieving low back pain, a pain cream made with mannitol, a natural sweetener that has been shown to shut down the main pain, itch and inflammation receptor on nerves, how to use Kleenex and duct tape to make orthotics for people with foot and knee pain and many others.

If you would like more info on any of Dr. Bertrand's studies, modalities or natural pain remedies, please contact her at:

Email: qrcream3@gmail.com
Website: https://QRcream.com
LinkedIn: https://www.linkedin.com/in/hélène-bertrand-12742a1a
Facebook: https://www.facebook.com/helene.bertrand.940
QR Cream: https://www.facebook.com/QRCream
Instagram: https://www.instagram.com/qrcream

Visit this page for a video demonstration of the 2-minute back pain relief exercise: https://drhelenebertrand.com

CHAPTER THREE

Create Harmony Within to Maximize Success Without
By Chanie Twersky

The Hidden Key to Leadership

Imagine if the key to unlocking your full leadership potential was something hidden in plain sight.

What if the secret to your success is hidden in the very foundation of who you are?

Conscious leaders and entrepreneurs understand that relationships within a business are crucial for the success and achievement of their goals. However, what leaders may not realize is the identity of their company's most valuable relationship—the one that can impact all other relationships as well as influence overall success.

You might ask, "What relationship is that? And what makes it the most important one of all?"

Take a moment and imagine walking into your office on a Monday morning. Looking around, you think about everything you need to do and of the various people involved in your business. You might think about your secretary, your board of directors (if you have one), or maybe even the maintenance guy who needs to fix your copier!

While it seems obvious that all relationships are vital for overall success, I found within my 30+ year leadership journey that there is one relationship that supersedes them all. Interestingly, it is not commonly recognized or spoken about. It has been a blessing for me to learn this and I now wish to pass it on to you.

That ever-important relationship is the one with your "inner child."

Have you ever heard of this term?

You might already be familiar with the concept of emotional intelligence and its significance in business operations. This goes one step further.

"Inner child," or how I like to refer to as inner children, refers to our original, authentic self. It harbors our early emotional experiences, both positive and negative and the wellspring for our joy, creativity, and innocence.

Your early experiences impact your present decisions, temperament and leadership style, more than you might realize. Transforming your relationship with yourself and your inner children will optimize your leadership potential.

Your inner children are YOU. Every moment of your past is still alive within you.

This is good news when you know how to relate to them.

The Inner Children Relationship (ICR) Quadrant

You can forge a loving relationship with your inner family in a way where you will notice a powerful shift in your leadership. Let's first assess how you presently relate to your inner child.

Here is a quick and easy self-assessment tool that I developed to help leaders identify how they relate to their inner children.

As a wise mentor once shared: "self-awareness is half the journey to resolution."

The Inner Children Relationship (ICR) Quadrant categorizes the ways we relate to our inner family.

These 4 common approaches are based on what we have learned early on to care, or not to care, for our feelings. How we treat ourselves now is reflected in how we were treated as children.

The ICR Quadrant:

- Hush: Silencing our inner children when they express pain or discomfort.

- Avoid: Pretending these (inner) younger versions of you don't exist.

- Reject: Being critical or harsh towards our inner experiences.

- Embrace: Acknowledging and nurturing our inner children's needs and feelings.

It is common to fluctuate among these 4 ways of being, especially before we understand the impact of this relationship in our lives.

Further in this chapter, I share with you a practical tool that will guide you in how to more effectively embrace those little boys and girls who are living within you. That newly found bond will be the secret key to your leadership success!

Backed by Science

Recent studies* indicate that over 85% of adult behavior is rooted in our experiences between the ages of 0–7. Those are inner children frozen in time that cannot grow up unless you know how to embrace and integrate them into your present life. Freeing them restores your most authentic and full expression of you. You don't need to be a therapist or even go to therapy to set yourself up so that your unattended inner children do not screw up your business or life. There are ways to learn and master the skills needed to harmonize within, retroactively embracing you in every moment of the past and unleashing the rock star leader in you.

Heal and Succeed

In January 2012, when I was at the dawn of a major personal transformational era, I was graced to be introduced to leaders like Clair Zammit. I remember hearing this beautiful woman, founder of Feminine Power and Evolving Wisdom, tell the story of how she felt invisible growing up as a child. Healing the little girl who felt invisible was the groundwork for all her successes which includes founding one of the fastest growing transformational schools in the world.

"I knew I had a contribution to make, I knew I had gifts and talents, but I had no idea how to create a life that fully expressed them," Claire Zammit said. She found the key in reclaiming her inner children. You too have the keys to manifest your dreams!

My Story: An Unconventional Journey

There was always a leader in me although it took a long journey to embody the quality of leadership I sought. I started as a high school teacher, where I lived within the confines of a life that was mostly chosen for me.

Married at 18 without meeting my husband and subsequently giving birth to eight children, I followed cultural norms without question. But deep inside, a crisis was brewing—a crisis that became my awakening.

After years of talk therapy, with a deteriorating marriage, and the birth of my eighth child, I hit rock bottom. I was lost, frightened, and trapped. It was then that I awakened into my truth and forged the path back home to myself. That included healing my inner family.

My crisis and awakening inspired my ultimate leadership. I stepped into my peak leadership as a mom to a large family, as a growing influencer and leader—especially in the parenting arena and in leading my own life—expanding into the fullness of who I am today.

Stepping Stones

The three steps to help you get there are: education, commitment, and support.

Education:

Understanding childhood trauma and how we function as emotional beings is crucial for our growth as leaders. It can otherwise lead us to fall into patterns we have learned early on in life which turns into defensive leadership traits like micromanaging or avoiding, which can stem from an underlying need for control or fear of being vulnerable.

It's essential to learn more about it and recognize that our reactions and experiences are normal, allowing us to approach them with compassion and curiosity.

Commitment:

Knowledge alone is insufficient. It's about recognizing that your inner children are not just metaphors; they are the living memories within you. They are you. Every moment in the past is still alive within you. There are ways to relate to them, care for them and heal them.

Caring for your inner family is part of prioritizing your self-care, as a leader's well-being sets the tone for the entire organization.

Support:

Create a network of support where you don't do this alone. Hire a mentor and surround yourself with others already doing similar work. In my journey, it was critical to say yes to every lifeboat the universe sent my way.

A network of support isn't just about having people to turn to; it's about creating an environment where vulnerability is seen as a strength and personal growth is a shared goal.

Recognize and Embrace Them

Integrating the inner child is not about digging up the past, but about honoring the full spectrum of your inner experiences and allowing them to coexist with your adult self in harmony.

Think of a leadership challenge you're facing. When was the last time you felt a strong emotional reaction at work? How might your inner child's needs play a role in any of this?

I created a practical tool that builds upon the ICR Quadrant and is designed to help you recognize your inner child and more easily access and embrace them.

Are you ready to move from hushing, ignoring and rejecting to finally make peace and embrace them all?

Using a tool I have created—the 5-Petaled FLAIR Emotions Chart—you can recognize your underlying emotions.

FLAIR is an acronym for Frightened, Lost, Abandoned, Ignored, and Rejected—emotions children experience when still dependent on adult caregivers.

For example, a child who is treated in less-than-nurturing ways will feel *frightened* and fear for their life and survival. That emotion is reasonable for an infant and young child. Since they truly are wholly dependent and cannot survive without parental care.

Have you ever seen an infant's body language reflect that intense fear?

These early childhood emotions and reactions to life experiences change as we mature into independent and interdependent adults. If others neglect us or are harsh with us, our survival won't be threatened.

However, a reminder of past experiences is enough to trigger an intense feeling or sense of threat and the strong reaction will stem from the younger you.

Using the FLAIR Chart, you can find the healing your inner child needs to counter those intense emotions. Doing this process can help you feel empowered in your leadership.

The counter emotions to FLAIR are:

Frightened ~ Safe

Lost ~ Guided

Abandoned ~ Cared For

Ignored ~ Valued

Rejected ~ Loved and Accepted Unconditionally

Below is a link to download a visual image of the chart.

Practice Exercise:

Let's explore how to use the FLAIR Chart to help you overcome common triggers and potential pitfalls in your business. Allow me to offer three examples where you can test the application of this method.

> **Example 1**: You have multiple projects on your list. And on top of that, your boss, or if you're the boss, you, are expecting to have them done by a nearing deadline.
>
> Your initial reaction: Overwhelm.
>
> Your secondary reaction: Procrastinating and distracting yourself with irrelevant activities like binge scrolling or eating.
>
> From the FLAIR Chart perspective: You are feeling *lost*.

In my childhood, I felt lost much of the time. My mother had 13 children besides me, and I needed to learn life on my own from when I was a toddler. That childhood wound is still with me.

It is natural for a young child to feel lost. They are still learning every tiny step of life. Embracing your lost inner child will calm them. You can become their ultimate guide to show them and teach them how to live life. And that will help you respond to your tasks from the resourceful adult leader self.

Example 2: Your employee or business partner raised his voice with you, criticizing, blaming, and used harsh words.

You might naturally react in this way: Fear and hurt.

Other reactions: You may have fantasies of how you can take revenge and hurt the one who raised their voice to you or promise yourself to never talk to them again.

I was bullied as a young girl into my teens and every time I am mistreated, those bullied younger selves are triggered and I feel unsafe. Learning how to provide safety retroactively to younger Chanie's has helped me deal with challenging relationships and circumstances in my business.

Let's look at it through the FLAIR lens: You're feeling frightened.

A young child needs to feel safe as a baseline. Feeling attacked in your adult life can cause your younger selves to feel unsafe and threatened. If you can identify *that*, you can immediately connect inwardly and find the younger "you's" who are feeling frightened. And what will you as an adult provide to your scared inner child? Yes, a feeling of safety and protection. Only you can offer that to them. Can you notice how embracing your inner family can potentially help prevent ugly conflicts in your business?

Example 3: Your employee did something in the business without asking or letting you know beforehand. However, the step they took was beneficial for the business.

Here is how you might react: Anger.

Other thoughts and feelings: You feel disrespected, unacknowledged, and unimportant in your worker's eyes. You have planned and thought to fire them, even though they are great for the company because you do not tolerate being treated as if they are the boss and you are nothing.

> *Being one of fourteen children left me feeling like I was a fly on the wall that saw everything but was not noticed. It took healing my inner child all the way to infancy to build a solid sense of self. This healing has turned me into a confident leader, and you can do that too.*

In the FLAIR Language, you feel: Ignored.

A young child who is disregarded much of the time can lose their natural sense of self. They need their caretakers to reflect in them their preciousness and value. When you can go inside and embrace all the little "you's" who grew up being ignored in those young delicate years and allow them to see that you see their value, you will shift those early self-esteem wounds.

Healing Hack

Every emotional discomfort is an opportunity to build your relationship with the younger versions of you. They all are you—and you can build a solid relationship within that will reflect on the outside. The more time, energy, and attention you invest in your inner family, the more harmony you will experience as a leader, diminishing internal and external chaos or distress.

Using the information and tools in this chapter can help you shift your leadership quality at lightning speed. The 5-Petal FLAIR Chart can help you recognize your inner family and what your inner child might need in response to their triggered pain. And the ICR can remind you how you want to relate to them.

This inner work will keep you ahead of the game. Educating yourself, committing to this valuable inner relationship, and building the right support system will bring you the results you seek.

Download the FLAIR chart and ICR tool and keep it near your working space for easy reference and practice when needed.

https://peakleaderships.com/book-photos

If you want to take this further, you are welcome to join our community and program.

In my Peak Leadership Program, I go deeper into each of the categories, and I include a specialized practice that turbocharges the healing experience. Doing this work can be the quantum leap you seek toward your dreams in your business and life.

Chanie Twersky is a mother of eight. She descends from a long line of historic leaders, such as the Baal Shem Tov, the founders of Hassidic teachings in the 1700's, including the concepts of what is now known as the law of attraction and other advanced personal growth wisdom. She was arranged at a young age to marry someone from that same lineage and needed to learn how to emerge from the challenges that came with it. Her own journey led her to train and apprentice with leading-edge trauma experts, which helped shape her amazing leadership and parenting expertise. She is the founder of the Peak Parenting Academy, a supportive place for conscious professionals who are looking to start a family. She has helped hundreds of people transform their leadership in their families and at work.

Email: chanie@chanietwersky.com

Website: https://peakleaderships.com
LinkedIn: https://www.linkedin.com/in/chanie-twersky-b7025037
Instagram: https://www.instagram.com/chanie_twersky

* Bruce Lipton among other scientists

Join us here:

CHAPTER FOUR

AI: The Secret Weapon for Small Business Success
By Sandy Sandler

"Artificial intelligence is about to accelerate the rate of new innovation discoveries at a pace we've never seen before." —Bill Gates

Have you ever wished for an employee who never complains, never sleeps, never takes a sick day, and never asks for a paycheck? Well, I have several … they're called artificial intelligence (AI) tools.

My journey with AI began hesitantly. I was not a tech enthusiast, in fact, I always referred to myself as "clinically technophobic!" But, kicking and screaming (no … not really), I agreed to attend an AI class in 2022 and, to my surprise, I immediately realized the potential of AI. It was explained to me that ChatGPT-3.5 was just like texting to a very smart friend. I thought, "Wow, even I could do that!"

My curiosity regarding AI grew and in March 2023, the release of ChatGPT-4 transformed the AI landscape with over 14,700 AI startups and over 100,000 AI tools. Most recently, in January 2024, Microsoft introduced Copilot Pro, a version built on ChatGPT-4, but Copilot Pro adds AI to the Microsoft Office suite of products. Soon after, in February 2024, Google introduced Gemini Advanced, a competing product to Copilot Pro, which works with the Google suite of apps.

This is only the beginning of the AI deluge, and I can't wait to see where it goes. I advise you to jump on the ship to ensure you are cruising the AI waters!

I'm thrilled to share my passion and professional insights on the incredible impact of AI on small businesses. To help you get over any reservations you may have about these tools, I want to take you into this fascinating world where possibilities are endless.

I've personally used and fallen in love with numerous AI tools that can transform your small business, but I will share four tools in this chapter: ChatGPT-4, Copilot Pro, Descript, and MidJourney.

ChatGPT-4 and the Newer Version of Copilot Pro Are Amazing!

ChatGPT-4, with its latest release in March 2023, has been an AI game-changer. It's like finding a treasure trove of helpful insights. I prefer the paid version because, as one of my AI mentors told me, the free version is like "drunk ChatGPT." ChatGPT-4 can assist with copywriting, blogging, title generation, product descriptions and even video transcription while ensuring SEO optimization.

Descript: An AI Video Editor

Descript is a revolutionary tool for video editing. It transcribes your videos or podcasts, making them as easy to edit as a Word document. It even magically eliminates filler words like "um."

MidJourney: The Artistic AI

MidJourney has a steeper learning curve, but it's a creative powerhouse. It can generate stunning images in various styles, from photorealistic to Pixar-type styles, to blended images and so much more, making it a favorite among artists and graphic designers. We even used it for Bowdabra product packaging photos. The images were incredible, looking as if we hired professional models, set designers and photographers, but I used only MidJourney to create them. Truly amazing!

More Examples of AI's Role in Small Business Success

Small businesses face the challenge of attracting customers and managing operations efficiently. AI isn't just a tool; it's like a co-worker or an employee who can work tirelessly to boost efficiency, spark imagination and even open new doors.

AI can also act as a marketing expert, creating engaging content and handling repetitive tasks, which leads to saving valuable time for business owners. It also can create numerous different types of marketing pieces, from flyers to squeeze pages.

AI's Impact Beyond Marketing

AI transforms various aspects of business operations, from customer service to inventory management, providing invaluable insights for better decision-making. It can even write computer code, landing pages and more.

Leading the Way with AI

Small businesses should be at the forefront of AI adoption, actively shaping a future where AI plays a crucial role—not just following the trend but leading the way.

The Challenges and Transformations Brought by AI

There has been some controversy surrounding AI and its role in our world. My opinion is that AI isn't here to replace jobs but to transform them. I look at AI as a powerful virtual assistant that can increase efficiency, spark innovation, and create new opportunities. It needs us to help it learn and grow because it learns every time information is input. With millions of people using it every day, the AI is getting better and better.

Another challenge with AI is that it needs to get better at not "hallucinating," i.e., making things up. Therefore, it is always imperative that you fact-check research or answers that AI provides to you to be certain that it didn't give you false information. One trick is to ask AI to give you the resources for the information it provides to you. Also, there is a tool called perplexity.ai, which is like Google on steroids, and it will always give you resources for information that it provides.

Transforming Jobs with AI

AI can assist in numerous tasks, making them more efficient, from creating product designs to streamlining processes.

AI is not just a tool for automating tasks, but it also serves as a catalyst for growth and creativity. AI has the potential to make various tasks more efficient—such as designing products or streamlining processes. However, its genuine ability to bring about profound transformation lies in its capacity to enhance skills, nurture collaborations and facilitate the generation of innovative insights and solutions.

AI as an Intelligent Assistant

One of the ways in which AI can revolutionize jobs is by acting as an assistant that supports us mere mortals in performing our tasks more effectively and efficiently. For instance, AI can aid doctors in diagnosing diseases, support lawyers in contract review, help teachers personalize learning experiences, or assist journalists with fact-checking. Additionally, AI can provide feedback suggestions and reminders to enhance the quality and accuracy of work. By delegating repetitive aspects of our jobs to AI systems, we can devote our attention to intricate and creative aspects that demand real human judgment and intuition.

AI as a Collaborative Partner

Another transformation brought about by AI is its ability to enable forms of collaboration between humans and machines, as well as among humans themselves.

AI is a valuable tool in creative processes, such as image creation and storytelling, by saving time and enhancing quality.

For instance, AI has the potential to enhance the design process for engineers, aiding in the generation and evaluation of alternative designs. Similarly, architects can utilize AI to optimize building plans based on criteria leading to new ideas or designs. Moreover, artists can explore realms of creativity by combining mediums and styles with the help of AI. Additionally, AI can greatly facilitate communication and coordination amongst teams by offering services such as translation, transcription, summarization and calendar syncing. By collaborating with AI technologies, humans can harness their strengths alongside those of AI to achieve outcomes that would be challenging for them to attain individually.

AI also possesses the ability to act as an innovator by uncovering patterns, insights and solutions that may not have been considered by humans. It serves as a catalyst for inspiration and encourages individuals to think beyond boundaries while exploring fresh possibilities from numerous different perspectives. Through learning from AI systems, humans are capable of expanding their knowledge base and imagination while fostering a culture that values change and embraces experimentation. To put it simply, AI enhances capabilities and helps you work smarter and faster.

I have been able to harness these AI tools to make my business more adaptable, dynamic, and innovative. The key takeaway here is that AI tools are not about automating everything; rather, they enhance all our abilities, our efficiency and our capacity for transformation.

An Overview of the Multiple Ways AI Can Impact Your Business

In the realm of customer service, AI chatbots can handle simple customer inquiries while effectively freeing up your team to address the more complex issues promptly.

With inventory management, AI can predict stock requirements accurately, preventing both overstocking and understocking.

It is as though you have a magical crystal ball that reveals hidden insights into your inventory!

AI also has the potential to greatly assist in financial management tasks. With the help of AI tools, you can streamline your bookkeeping processes to efficiently manage invoices and even benefit from financial forecasting capabilities. This becomes particularly invaluable for small businesses like mine, where resources are often limited. In essence, AI is revolutionizing the way we conduct business—from automating tasks to providing insights and predictions. It's important to note that this transformation is not about technology taking over; instead, it is about empowering us.

Many people express concerns about AI taking our jobs. I believe that AI is here to transform our work and create opportunities rather than to replace us. It's about enhancing what we do.

Certainly, there will be jobs that AI can automate. Tasks like data entry or analysis can be done efficiently by AI. But this doesn't necessarily mean job loss; it means that jobs will evolve. Similar to the industrial revolution, the workforce will need to adapt and acquire new skills.

For instance, paralegals who embrace AI tools can now focus more on analyzing cases, rather than spending countless hours on repetitive research tasks. Similarly, in the field of medicine, AI assists doctors in making diagnoses without replacing them; it enhances their abilities and expertise.

In my experience, I have witnessed how AI unlocks possibilities for creativity and innovation.

I am so excited by how AI is helping my business. At Bowdabra, we have integrated AI into our designs, enabling us to explore marketing strategies that were previously unimaginable.

AI tools have improved the efficiency of my operations while also opening new avenues for creative vision, not only for me, but for my Bowdabra design team members as well.

Indeed, it is true that AI will impact jobs, but I believe that AI also presents new opportunities. The key is to embrace these changes and perceive them as potential for growth. By being adaptable and open to acquiring new skills and viewing AI as a virtual assistant, AI can propel you to new heights in either your professional career or your small business growth. As you become more familiar with AI, you will discover its potential to assist in many aspects of your business.

I can't encourage you enough to explore AI tools. You might be hesitant like I was at first, but start small, begin with one task and you'll see how impactful AI is.

Start by using AI Tools for personal and simple professional tasks. Use the free version of Copilot and ask it to create a meal plan, or a vacation plan, or even let your kids use it as a math, science or English tutor. You will become addicted!

Learn prompt engineering to communicate effectively with AI. "Prompt engineering" sounds extremely technical, but it is just the information that you type into the AI. The more effective the prompt, the better the information that AI will give you. Essentially, you are just typing to AI as if you are texting to a very smart colleague. Treat the AI as if it were a human virtual assistant. If you don't give your assistant the correct information, your assistant won't deliver you the finished results that you want. If you would like some examples of different types of prompts, please use this QR code below for a guide to getting started in chatting with AI.

Embracing AI is not a trend; it's a necessity for small businesses and other professionals. My journey and the success stories I've heard from others show how AI can transform leadership and business operations. Small business owners can harness the power of AI to stay competitive, save time and reach new heights of success.

Sandy Sandler is the visionary entrepreneur behind the Bowdabra®. With her innovative bow-making tool, she has empowered craft enthusiasts worldwide. Sandy is a champion of business empowerment, teaching small business owners how to utilize artificial intelligence tools for personal and professional growth. She also fosters dogs and mentors college students, making a profound impact in both the marketplace and the lives of others. To contact Sandy, please reach out to her at:

Email: FreeAIGift@sandysandler.com
Website: www.sandysandler.com
LinkedIn: https://www.linkedin.com/in/sandysandler

CHAPTER FIVE

From Resilience to Revelation: A Journey in Elder Care Leadership
By Jenny Ferguson

As I sit down to share my story, I'm struck by the serendipitous twists of fate that have shaped my journey. My current role as the owner of CA Senior Care Consulting, a thriving elder care consulting company, was a path I neither predicted nor planned. Yet, here I am, a testament to life's unpredictable nature and the power of passion and resilience.

Embracing the Unexpected

My journey into the elder care industry began during a period of profound personal challenges. Like many, I was unprepared for the complexities and emotional toll of navigating long-term care for an aging loved one, in this case my dad. The statistics are startling: 70% of Americans will require some form of long-term care as they age, yet only a fraction are financially prepared for this inevitability. I laid awake at night worrying about how we were going to pay for the care he needed, but also not knowing exactly what kind of care he needed. That saying "you don't know what you don't know" never rang truer. I felt lost and uncertain of how to start this necessary process. It was a period marked by frustration, fear, guilt and an overwhelming sense of responsibility.

The Foundations of My Leadership

Reflecting on my life, certain qualities have consistently defined me: resilience, kindness, competitiveness, intelligence and a relentless work ethic. These traits were evident from my childhood as I was passionate about sports and fiercely competitive at everything I did. A pivotal moment came when, at eight years old, I discovered my love for ice skating. Despite the financial strain it placed on my modest, middle-class family, my parents supported my passion, setting me on a path that taught me discipline, dedication and the pursuit of excellence. God bless them.

My father's lifelong battle with hydrocephalus, a condition he fought valiantly against with over 21 brain surgeries, instilled in me an early understanding of resilience. At one point, after he miraculously came out of a lengthy coma, watching him relearn basic daily activities and maintain his humor and love despite his challenges was profoundly impactful. My mother's unwavering support for our family—as she returned to school to become a nurse while juggling the roles of caregiver, mother and breadwinner—was another pillar of strength that shaped my character.

From Ice Rinks to Real Estate: The Evolution of a Leader

My journey took many turns—from being a competitive ice skater, to a professional ice skater, to a skating coach, then simultaneously venturing into real estate while raising my daughters, Haley and Mia. Each phase brought new challenges and learnings, shaping my approach to leadership and life. My mother's sudden passing in 2009 was a pivotal moment, forcing me to confront the fragility of life, the feelings of profound loss and grief while remaining strong, and the complexities of taking over new responsibilities.

Stepping into Elder Care

The real turning point in my life and career came with my father's health decline 10 years later. Navigating the elder care system for him was overwhelming and eye-opening. I realized the dire need for compassionate, knowledgeable guidance in this field. This experience sparked a fire in me, leading me to pivot my career towards elder care.

The decision to transform my father's home into an elder care facility was both an emotional and a strategic move. It was a way to honor his legacy and address the gap I saw in the elder care industry. It gave me a chance to provide a space I would have wanted him to be in the last few months of his life. I embarked on this journey with passion and determination, navigating the complexities of licensing and administration with no prior experience in this sector.

Leading with Heart and Purpose

Owning and running an elder care facility was a profound experience. I fell in love with it. It taught me the importance of empathy, personalized care, and the impact of creating a nurturing environment for the elderly. I felt like a mom to my residents, wanting nothing but the very best for them all day, every day. This period also brought clarity to my role in the elder care industry. I realized my true calling lay in directly assisting families and individuals navigating the elder care maze.

During the COVID pandemic, I faced another crucial decision point. I sold the care home but knew my journey in elder care was far from over. I took up a role with a local hospice company as a hospice care consultant, which broadened my understanding of the industry. So many new pieces to the elder care puzzle were learned: insurance coverage, skilled nursing and rehab stays, discharge planning, etc. However, I missed the direct interaction with families, which led me to establish CA Senior Care Consulting.

California Senior Care Consulting: A Dream Realized

Starting CASCC was a culmination of all my experiences, learnings, and passions. It allowed me to leverage my expertise to guide families through the daunting process of elder care planning and decision-making. I specialize in assisted living and memory care placement; however, I feel I am a great source for people who may just need guidance and support. My approach is deeply personal—I've been in their shoes, felt their frustrations and understand their fears.

My Leadership Philosophy

Reflecting on my journey, I see leadership not just as a position but as a way of being. True leadership is about inspiring and empowering others, leading by example and staying true to one's values. It's about turning challenges into opportunities for growth and learning. My leadership has always been heart-centered, guided by empathy, resilience and a relentless drive to make a positive impact.

Embracing Change and Following Your Dreams

Life has taught me the value of being open to change and the power of following your heart, even if it leads you down an unexpected path. My journey from a figure skater to a real estate agent, and now to an elder care consultant and public speaker, is a testament to this belief.

Looking Ahead

As I continue on this path, my mission remains clear: to educate, support and guide others through the complexities of elder care. The challenges are many, but the rewards of helping others navigate this critical phase of life are immeasurable.

A Call to Action

To those facing the challenges of elder care, I urge you to be proactive, ask the hard questions, and prepare for the future. I have a flyer available listing the five most important things to do now for our aging loved ones. If you would like a copy, please email me and request one. And to those on their own journey of discovery and growth, I encourage you to embrace the unexpected, follow your heart and lead with purpose. Remember, leadership is not just about where you are going; it's about who you become along the way.

Jenny Ferguson is the owner and CEO of CA Senior Care Consulting. Jenny has worn many hats along her journey to this point: competitive ice skater turned professional ice skater, realtor, owner and administrator of an assisted living home, a hospice care consultant, and now she specializes in long-term care placement and consulting. She also has recently added bestselling author and keynote speaker to her resume. To book Jenny as a speaker or discuss generational leadership in the workplace, please contact her at:

Email: jenny@cascc.me
Website: https://www.cascc.me
LinkedIn: https://www.linkedin.com/in/jenny-ferguson-78bb01269
Instagram: ca_senior_care_consulting

CHAPTER SIX

Leadership in Crisis—Stepping Up When Destiny Calls
By Nigel J. Smart, PhD

In the art of leadership, opportunities can often present themselves at the most unexpected times from the most unusual places. I want to share aspects of things I have learned that have helped to develop me at key moments in my life. It's my belief that these occasions have propelled my progress and helped to shape my life destiny.

Before we delve into the heart of this story, I want to introduce you to a valuable tool I employed during my journey—a tool that can help you navigate challenges and define your purpose as a leader. It's called the 7 Level Deep Tool. We'll revisit this tool later in the story, but for now, let me introduce it to you so you can keep it in mind as we explore the remarkable journey I'm about to share.

If you are a parent, understand that the most important things you want for your children are their well-being, their happiness and their success. But why is that important?

I want you to ask yourself the question and give it some thought so you can come up with a true reason and motivation for your answer. Once you've done that, ask yourself the same question again, but dig a little deeper this time so that you can go to the next level of thought and emotion. When you do this, you'll feel the reasoning change and the emotions you experience will be enhanced. "Why is that?" you ask. It's because you are starting to dig into the real core reasons why you make your choices. This is something that is important to know (it's a MUST), as it will play into how you will make your decisions as a leader.

For the complete experience, I want you to repeat the process seven times (7 Levels Deep), taking note each time you complete a cycle.

This will be a significant experience for you and it was massive in the way it affected my choices, so enjoy the process because it will be quite revealing.

My hope is that you will become aware of who you need to be today in order to recognize the moment when it's time to step up and meet the challenge that lies before you. For me, that defining moment arrived shortly after the birth of my son, Jonathan—an event that marked a turning point in my life's journey.

It was a challenge I neither needed nor wanted when it first appeared, but destiny was calling, and it became my duty to step forward and perform. This challenge proved to be both life-changing and character-enhancing, and I hope it will captivate your imagination and offer valuable lessons in leadership.

This is a story about leadership during a crisis and how I met my personal challenge to fulfill a specific need at a time of national turmoil. This story involves my experiences connected to the 9/11 attacks by Al-Qaeda, which led to my role in heading up the manufacturing of the anthrax vaccine for the military, supporting the impending invasion of Iraq and Afghanistan by the U.S. military in 2003.

As I share these experiences, I hope you'll be able to connect with my emotions and derive insights from my actions, preparing you for your own leadership challenges as you develop your unique style of leadership. My aspiration is that my story inspires you to embrace challenges and responsibilities, often arising unexpectedly.

The key to your success will be developing the necessary skills, ensuring you are ready to step up when the opportunity arises. Moreover, my greater purpose here is to initiate a chain reaction of leadership potential that inspires others to emulate your leadership experiences. This is a higher purpose—a sustainable mechanism for the future.

But before we delve into my story, let's first explore what I believe are the fundamentals of leadership and how they are influenced by various factors.

What is Leadership?

Leadership is an intangible quality that can be hard to define precisely, but it is a skill that can be learned. This is crucial because it means that leadership is inclusive—it's available to anyone who commits to its development.

Leadership is not a divine right; it's a lifelong process that evolves through experiences. You don't wake up one morning as a leader; it's something you grow into. Leadership separates those who become leaders from those who follow leaders. What identifies and distinguishes leadership qualities?

Some core elements of leadership include:

- **Confidence and Self-Belief:** A leader possesses confidence and belief in their own capabilities, even if they initially lack belief.
- **Inspiring Others:** Leaders ignite the imagination of others and create momentum where there was none.
- **Openness to Input:** They are willing to listen to others' opinions and accept criticism after making unpopular decisions.
- **Resourcefulness:** Leaders can acquire the necessary resources to achieve defined goals and objectives.

Leaders step up when others may fear the way forward and stand strong, even when faced with uncertainty and vulnerability. They focus on objectives and what is right, not driven by popularity. Leadership demands making tough choices and staying the course, even when the journey becomes challenging. It's about bringing others along with your vision and having the credibility to acquire the resources needed to succeed.

Effective leaders have strong interpersonal skills and can rally a team for the journey ahead. To empower a group, fostering a team spirit and clarity of purpose are vital. Popularity is not a prerequisite, but a sense of collectiveness—and this harmony enhances the likelihood of achieving collective goals.

Leadership cannot coexist with arrogance; authenticity and action are crucial. Leaders must lead by example, and actions must align with principles, belief systems, and philosophies. Fine oratory can be impressive initially, but authenticity prevails in the long run. Leaders must have skin in the game to garner respect.

Leaders recognize their limits, seek compatibility with others, and encourage active participation to maximize success. They remain composed and nonreactive in the face of challenges, able to compartmentalize issues to neutralize conflicts while harnessing passion appropriately. They understand the importance of listening, removing obstacles, and seeking perspectives outside their immediate circle.

Mistakes are part of leadership, but the key is learning from those mistakes. Leaders grow through experience and maintain a positive mindset, even during challenging times. Post-mortems are necessary but should not turn into a blame culture. Inclusiveness, patience and adaptability are essential for success, along with a commitment to fundamental principles: integrity, honesty, and competitiveness.

These principles provide guidance, ensuring that leaders stay on course, maintain group belief, and sustain momentum for growth.

Now, let me share my story—the "Anthrax Vaccine Production Experience."

In 2001, I had just become a father to my son Jonathan, and I was relishing the opportunity to spend time at home with him. The world was on edge, with President George W. Bush recently elected, and global events taking unexpected turns. I had experience in military vaccine-related initiatives, so when I was asked to help resolve manufacturing issues in Michigan, it wasn't entirely unexpected.

However, due to personal circumstances, I initially declined the assignment, prioritizing time with my son. Little did I know that destiny had other plans.

On September 11, 2001, the world witnessed the horrific 9/11 attacks. As I watched the events unfold on TV, I knew that life was about to change. The phone rang again, asking for my help.

The next day, I made the difficult decision to leave my family behind and answer the call for assistance. I understood the gravity of the situation and knew it was my duty to step up.

My journey began with a car ride to the airport at 4:30 a.m., followed by an eerie flight with only a handful of passengers and a tense flight crew. I arrived at my destination, where military guards and barbed wire surrounded the facility.

The mission: to re-license the vaccine factory with the FDA and establish reliable production. The facility and process were in poor shape and morale was low.

Over the next weeks, I focused on addressing licensing issues and collaborated with consultants. The FDA-releasable product was far less than reported and the process was inconsistent. I knew changes were needed to pass the FDA inspection and this would require strong communication and collaboration.

I was soon asked to take over leadership of the production team, which required a reorganization. This wasn't popular but it was necessary. I presented my plan to the CEO and announced it at an all-hands meeting. The response was overwhelming, demonstrating the importance of having a clear vision and inspiring others.

We faced challenges with the production process but I used tools like the 54321 technique to gather my thoughts and the language augmentation tool to improve communication. Listening was crucial to address objections and maintain team confidence.

I chose young, impressionable scientists to lead and used visualization to motivate them. We had to address issues with the production train, which required a halt in production runs. Communication and negotiation were key as we made necessary changes.

In the end, our dedication and hard work paid off. Manufacturing resumed and we produced the best-quality vaccine ever. The impact on team morale was significant and we celebrated our achievement.

In conclusion, my story illustrates the tools and techniques you can employ as a leader to overcome challenges. The 7 Level Deep Tool was instrumental in crystallizing my purpose during a crisis, allowing me to maintain focus and manage anxiety.

Leadership often requires personal commitment, especially in moments of national significance. My hope is that my journey inspires you to embrace challenges and responsibilities and develop the skills necessary to step up when opportunity arises.

Remember, leadership is not about having all the answers; it's about inspiring and guiding others toward a shared vision. It's about embracing core principles like integrity, honesty and competitiveness to stay the course, maintain momentum and achieve growth.

Nigel Smart is a serial entrepreneur with decades of experience in the biotechnology/pharmaceutical industry spanning both corporate and consulting situations. He is an international keynote speaker, multiple best-selling author and coach for corporations and individuals seeking to improve their levels of performance. He has provided key expert consulting to industry, the FDA and U.S. Department of Defense associated with systems to improve manufacturing quality issues, manufacturing efficiency and the production of anti-terrorist countermeasures. In relation to these issues, he has a special interest in the application of excellence principles and has developed the concept of POWERHOUSE LEADERSHIP to generate leadership qualities and high performance. Nigel is available to share these ideas as trainings and in-house sessions for your situations and can tailor custom applications for your individual circumstances.

Email: Nigel@Smartpharmaconsulting.com
Website: www.smartpharmaconsulting.com
LinkedIn: https://www.linkedin.com/in/nigel-smart-phd

CHAPTER SEVEN

Get to Know Yourself
By Angela Dingle

My passion lies in helping individuals unlock their true potential by getting to know themselves better. Over the years, I've had the privilege of guiding people on this transformative journey in various settings, from the corridors of government to boardrooms in Fortune 500 companies, from the spotlight of the stage to virtual rooms connecting individuals across the globe. If you're eager to enhance your confidence and expand your influence, I'm here with a plan to help you achieve just that.

Each year, I engage with people from all walks of life, including business executives, who often feel unheard, undervalued and powerless in their professional endeavors. It's a common thread that binds us—the experience of conflict. Did you know that a staggering 85% of employees, regardless of their position within an organization, encounter conflict to some degree? Conflict is an inevitable part of life. Despite our best efforts to avoid it, disagreements with others will arise. However, not all conflict is negative; some can be productive, leading to creative problem-solving. What truly matters is how we respond to conflict when it does occur. Conflict itself is unavoidable, but our responses can be either ineffective and harmful or effective and beneficial.

One of the greatest fears among managers is conflict management. When conflicts arise, individuals lacking the necessary skills often find themselves stumbling and struggling through the process. The primary sources of workplace conflict are personality clashes and ego clashes—situations where individuals oppose each other due to differing needs, wants, or values.

To expand your influence, you must effectively communicate who you are and what you aspire to achieve. You need the ability to inspire others to drive outcomes.

Step 1: Recognize and Respond—A Path to Self-Discovery

What are you striving to accomplish and what obstacles stand in your way? Do you feel the need to be someone else to succeed in the workplace? Do you believe you deserve a higher salary or a promotion but struggle to ask for it? Do you often feel that your voice goes unheard, only to be acknowledged when someone else voices the same idea? Are you continually acquiring new knowledge and skills but find yourself overlooked for high-visibility assignments?

I'm here to guide you on a journey of self-discovery that will enable you to achieve your goals. It all starts with recognizing and understanding your reactions to conflicts. When a situation triggers anger or frustration, you have a choice: react emotionally or respond thoughtfully. Some react emotionally, exacerbating the situation, while others may choose to avoid addressing the conflict altogether.

What if I told you that you can learn to recognize these triggering events and choose how you respond to conflict? Instead of avoiding it, raising your voice, or giving others the silent treatment, what if you could see the situation from their perspective?

Enter the Conflict Dynamics Profile® (CDP), a tool I use to teach people how to recognize and minimize conflict. It's an online assessment that helps you understand how conflicts unfold, identify behaviors that trigger emotional responses (your "hot buttons"), and learn strategies to de-escalate conflicts when they arise.

Step 2: The Power of Response

Imagine a situation that made you angry. How differently might it have turned out if you knew how to respond constructively? How has your reaction to others' behavior affected your ability to achieve your personal and professional goals? What might your career trajectory look like if you had the skills to manage conflict effectively?

Step 3: Real-World Success Stories

Let's delve into a few examples that highlight the effectiveness of the tools I advocate for:

- **Public Sector Leadership Development:** In the public sector, managing conflict is an essential component of career advancement. Government guidelines mandate leadership competency training, including conflict management, for aspiring supervisors and managers. Leadership Development Programs (LDP) incorporate assessments like the CDP to help individuals understand their personality types, leadership styles, and conflict resolution abilities. These initiatives aim to prepare leaders for various challenges, ensuring a pool of qualified candidates for leadership roles.

- **Private Sector Leading Change:** A case in point is the change in leadership at X (formerly Twitter), which led to significant conflicts and negative outcomes. Layoffs occurred abruptly, causing distress among employees. The emails announcing the layoffs were perceived as blunt and lacking detail, leading to further conflict. This situation illustrates the importance of effective leadership and conflict management in maintaining a positive work environment. Organizational assessments like the Business Identity Assessment help organizations understand a team's capacity for change and capacity to adapt as the business needs.

Step 4: The Challenge of Conflict

Conflict is a natural part of the workplace, given the diversity of values, goals, and perspectives among team members. Instead of attempting to eliminate conflict entirely, we should anticipate its occurrence and develop procedures to identify, define and manage it constructively. As leaders, we must acquire the skills necessary to engage others, make decisions in ambiguous situations, build relationships and handle conflicts effectively. Leadership training plays a crucial role in developing these abilities.

My own journey in leadership began with a warning: "It's not a matter of if you get sued, but when you get sued" over your actions as a leader. This sobering realization motivated me to explore self-discovery and conflict management further.

Step 5: The Impact of Conflict

Conflict consumes a significant portion of our professional lives, with employees in the United States. spending nearly three hours per week dealing with conflicts. Since the onset of the pandemic, remote and hybrid work environments have made conflict detection and resolution more challenging. Conflict can lead to personal attacks, illness, absenteeism, and project failures. Leadership skills, especially conflict management, are crucial in addressing these challenges. However, there is often a gap between managers' perceptions of their conflict-handling abilities and how their non-managerial peers perceive them.

Step 6: My Personal Journey

Let me share my personal journey—a reluctant hero's path to becoming an expert in leadership development. I started my career without envisioning myself standing on stages or writing chapters like this one. While working for a Fortune 500 company, I often found myself at odds with my colleagues. I advocated for what I believed was right, even when it meant going against the grain. However, my input was often disregarded, leading to feelings of being unheard and undervalued. This ongoing conflict eroded my confidence, prompting me to enhance my leadership skills.

I became a Certified Management Consultant (CMC), a licensed Myers-Briggs Type Indicator (MBTI) Practitioner and trained in administering leadership assessments like the CDP and others. These resources empowered me to be authentic, share my values, build strong relationships, and influence others.

Later in my career, I faced the challenging task of laying off employees during a reduction in force. While adhering to legal guidelines, I led with my values, providing support and guidance to those affected. Despite legal restrictions, I had the confidence to remain personable, caring and acted according to my values.

3 Steps to Get What You Want

To achieve your goals and expand your influence, follow these three steps:

Know Yourself: Take a self-assessment like the CDP to understand your personal style and behavior in various situations. Confidence is built on self-belief, and understanding yourself is the first step toward building that confidence.

Understand Your Values: Identify your core values and learn to convey their importance to others. Be willing to stand up for your values, even when it's challenging, as this is key to expanding your influence.

Stop Giving Away Your Power: Recognize your weaknesses, create plans for improvement, and hold yourself accountable. Build trust and credibility by admitting mistakes and taking responsibility. Your ability to inspire trust is a vital leadership quality.

Tools: Leadership Assessments

Leadership assessments like the CDP, MBTI, EQi and others provide deeper insights into your personal style and behaviors. These insights are invaluable in understanding your hot buttons and values, enabling you to set boundaries, respect diverse opinions and ultimately believe in yourself.

Case Studies: Applying the Tools for Success

I've had the privilege of working with organizations such as the U.S. Army Corp of Engineers (USACE) and the Department of Commerce, International Trade Administration, Global Markets. These organizations have used tools like the CDP to develop leadership skills, manage conflicts, and navigate complex challenges successfully.

Additionally, as a speaker and subject matter expert, I've shared insights on leadership, women in leadership, and cybersecurity with diverse audiences. My own experiences, coupled with research and practical advice, have culminated in my book, *Discovering Your Girl Powers: 10 Strategies to Build Confidence, Charisma, and Credibility*, which offers guidance for personal and professional growth.

I invite you to join my mastermind program, the Power of the Pact, where you can access one-on-one coaching, group accountability sessions, and an online community to support your journey to success.

In the end, remember that you have the power to shape your life and career. It's not about waiting for opportunities but creating them. Believe in yourself, stand for your values, and embrace the power of self-discovery to achieve your goals and expand your influence.

An award-winning business owner, Angela Dingle is the President and CEO of Ex Nihilo Management, LLC, a management and technology consultancy based in Washington, DC. Angela has worked with Fortune 500 companies, national nonprofits, state, local and Federal governments to help them achieve their strategic objectives. Using assessments, individualized coaching, mentoring and feedback, she helps leaders develop the confidence, clarity and behaviors necessary to achieve their professional and personal objectives.

- *Recipient, Enterprising Women of the Year Award, 2012*
- *Recipient, The American Small Business Coalition Eagle Spirit Award*
- *Recipient, Compuware Corporation's Profiles in Excellence Award*

- *Recipient, Data Computer Corporation of America's Presidential Award*
- *Top 25 Case Study Author, The Hot Momma's Project*
- *Participant in the Center for Women's Business Research, Accelerating the Growth of Businesses Owned by Women of Color*
- *Featured Guest on Federal News Radio's Women in Government Series*
- *Speaker, Woman Behind the Business (WBB) Retreat*
- *Featured Guest, WBB Talk Radio Program*
- *Contributing Author, Washington Technology Magazine*
- *Contributing Author, myContracting Magazine*
- *Speaker, "Cool Women, Hot Jobs" Career Day, The Young Women's Leadership School*
- *Mentor, FIRST Robotics Competition, Theodore Roosevelt SHS*

Angela is a Certified Management Consultant (CMC) and is a Myers Briggs Type Indicator (MBTI) Certified Practitioner. She holds a Master of Science in Management Information Systems from Bowie State University, a Bachelor of Science in Computer Science from DeVry University in Columbus, OH. Angela is a member of ISACA and Delta Sigma Theta Sorority, Inc. To contact Angela, please reach out to her at:

Address: 80 M ST SE, Suite 100, Washington, DC 20003
Email: adingle@exnihilo-mgmt.com
Phone: 202-379-4884
Website: www.discoveringyourpowers.com
Website: https://powerpact.lpages.co/power-pact-90-day-challenge
Facebook: angelacdingle
Instagram: angelacdingle
LinkedIn: linkedin.com/in/angeladingle

CHAPTER EIGHT

Global Leadership by Design
By Dr. Kristina Wachter

Who is the first person to come to mind when you think of an influential leader? Why does that person stand out? How far reaching is that person's influence? Now consider this, who has had the most impact on shaping your life? In the world of leadership, there's an intriguing truth: it's not just reserved for the select few. Ordinary individuals, just like you and me, hold the remarkable ability to turn the commonplace into something exceptional.

Everyone can lead. While some people are formally designated as leaders, others naturally assume leadership through their actions and impact. We have the power to become leaders by personal design. In this chapter, I will provide you with the skill set you need to become a global leader using a tailor-made four-step approach, the Culture SPIN Method™. You have the potential to become a leader by design.

Jack Ma exemplifies influential leadership, rising from humble beginnings in China to build the global Alibaba empire. Despite rejections from Harvard and jobs like KFC, he remained committed to his vision. With minimal resources, he founded Alibaba, connecting Chinese manufacturers with global buyers. Through action-driven commitment and clear communication, he steered Alibaba through initial challenges to become a global giant in e-commerce and technology.

Influential leadership is defined by unwavering commitment, clear communication, and the capacity to establish meaningful connections. The true measure of leadership lies in actions, regardless of scale, focusing on the impact on others and the achieved outcomes. For global leaders, authentically bridging cultural divides is crucial to fulfilling the needs of all stakeholders.

Global leadership emerges when you actively forge connections across borders, embracing the diverse human side of business. This is the power of deliberate leadership by design.

To lead effectively, you must first act. But before taking action, it is essential to plan. However, planning alone is not enough. To achieve your goals, you need a strategy for creating meaningful connections with others. The Culture SPIN Method™ will guide you through this journey, ensuring you have the tools to lead adeptly while considering stakeholders and cultural context in variable circumstances.

Powerful leaders need to be flexible. Having a plan in place makes it easier to adjust when needed. I've had many leadership experiences, but one that stands out was during my first faculty-led position in a study-abroad program in Barcelona. Our planned flight to Paris was suddenly canceled and we were left without accommodations upon arrival. The responsibility to ensure the safe transition of 25 university students to their new destination fell on my shoulders. Errors were not an option; significant funds were at risk; our organization's reputation was hanging in the balance and panic was rising among the inexperienced travelers.

To navigate this crisis, I knew I needed to form alliances. Using the principles of the Culture SPIN Method™, I forged collaborative relationships in both Spain and France. These connections played a pivotal role in successfully resolving the predicament, ensuring the care of the London students and orchestrating intricate negotiations to secure alternative flight arrangements for the Barcelona group, ultimately landing them safely in Paris.

Thanks to my network in Paris, accommodations were arranged, culminating in an unforgettable evening at a charming bistro that showcased the city's culture—a treat for us all. The significance of our successful resolution was paramount to the stakeholders. It set the stage for success.

The foundation of global leadership lies in forging connections across borders, embracing the diverse human side of business. The Culture SPIN

Method™ provides you with cross-cultural competency tools to build bridges, expand your reach and influence others positively.

Your foundation is built on trust, dignity and respect—for yourself and others. It's also secured by human connection, bringing people together with a common desire to make things work. With a solid foundation, you can build a cultural bridge that allows parties to meet on common ground or step into another worldview, providing access to each party's way of doing business on opposite sides of the bridge.

Failure to recognize and bridge cultural divides can have significant consequences for businesses. The cost of relocating a management-level employee to a new country can range from $3 million to $5 million, and between 40% and 75% of such relocations fail, resulting in major losses. This high failure rate is often attributed to the lack of cultural assimilation and understanding of how to operate in new territories.

Furthermore, the turnover rate for those in international business is high, with estimates ranging between 62% and 80% after two years. This comes at a significant cost, as it takes two to three times an employee's base salary to train a replacement and cover the lost transition time. Developing global leadership skills, including cultural intelligence, is essential to combat this pattern.

Global leaders recognize the opportunities available in today's interconnected world. They work to build sustainable systems of connection among people within their sphere of influence, understanding that their impact can expand exponentially with border crossings based on trust, dignity and respect. Every person is in a leadership position as an ambassador of their organization and knowing how to navigate new and unusual circumstances is crucial.

Indra Nooyi, the former CEO of PepsiCo, is a prime example of a leader with a remarkable global perspective. She recognized the importance of tailoring products to suit local tastes and preferences, amplifying PepsiCo's market presence across the globe. Nooyi's approach emphasized diversity within the organization and a deep understanding of different cultures in diverse markets, steering PepsiCo towards unprecedented international success.

Effective global leaders must be willing to navigate ambiguous circumstances, embrace the unknown, and build collaborative cultural bridges. The Culture SPIN Method™ offers a concise toolkit to survive and thrive in the globalized business world. It starts with a clear vision, adapts to the situation at hand, assembles the necessary elements and facilitates safe passage across cultural divides.

The Culture SPIN Method™ is designed to transform your vision into action, providing sustainable results. It empowers you to lead with purpose and authenticity, bridging cultural divides with confidence and empathy. By following the four-step approach—Vision, Blueprint, Assembly, and Crossing the Bridge—you can become a confident and successful global leader.

Step One: Vision

Your leadership design begins with inspiration that draws on your unique leadership style and underlying motivations. This initial stage lays the groundwork for you to craft a custom framework that aligns with your distinct approach to leadership. You determine how to cultivate cultural competency and transform that into cultural intelligence to work to your advantage.

Initially, you will identify your motives, consider the scope of your influence, evaluate your choices, define your objectives clearly and reflect on personal development.

Next, craft a comprehensive strategy to align with your company's global development initiatives. This strategy will not only exemplify your leadership but also trigger your company's growth.

During her tenure as Apple's Senior VP of Retail, Angela Ahrendts crafted an engaging and culturally sensitive retail experience for Apple's global customers. Her leadership style merged innovation and cultural diversity, reshaping Apple's approach to brick-and-mortar stores, celebrating the distinct flavors of various local cultures while retaining Apple's essence.

Step Two: Create a Blueprint

The second step in the Culture SPIN Method™ is to develop a blueprint. This involves drafting your vision and refining it based on the situation at hand. You will identify the essential information required, survey the cultural terrain, and analyze each facet from both your perspective and the destination's perspective. Collaborate with relevant parties to create a multilayered understanding of the situation and assess your contributions and limitations.

Create a comprehensive inventory of resources necessary for building the cultural bridge and strategically arrange these elements for effective integration. This step is crucial in ensuring a strong foundation for successful execution.

Step Three: Assembly

The third step in the Culture SPIN Method™ is assembly. It involves systematically blending intangible and tangible elements to form a unified entity. You will delve into the depths of cultural codes and crucial elements essential to fortify the integrity of your cultural bridge. Map out a clear and detailed plan, laying out each step of your mission.

Along this path, you will cultivate significant connections, employing the knowledge you've gathered to erect a bridge that spans cultural divides. Your cultural savvy and communication hold the structure in place. Keep in mind that you will need to put your cultural intelligence through rigorous tests to ensure the integrity of the bridge before you begin the crossing.

Step Four: Bridge the Gap

The fourth and final step in the Culture SPIN Method™ is crossing the bridge to overcome cultural divides. This step involves crafting and implementing strategies that solidify the effectiveness of your cultural bridge, benefiting all parties involved. While navigating the bridge, consider how you apply your knowledge, ensuring its cultural relevance and fostering trust, dignity and respect along the way.

Assess the pivotal components contributing to a secure journey and recognize the opportune moments to encourage leadership, unity and independence in others. As an effective global leader, you will strategically determine the appropriate timing to step back, empowering others while keeping the bridge open for continual two-way crossings.

This step ensures connectivity and nurtures ongoing cultural exchange and mutual understanding for sustainable relationships.

Muhtar Kent, the former CEO of The Coca-Cola Company, successfully bridged the gap between Japanese traditional values and Western business strategies. He blended these cultural aspects to boost efficiency and profitability, making a notable impact on Nissan's history.

Strong global leaders recognize the importance of power dynamics in different cultures, plan their actions based on roles, behaviors, and attitudes, and develop an understanding of cultural codes and cultural capital. They learn about the values and beliefs of the cultures they interact with, creating a foundation of trust and understanding.

Effective global leaders are collaborative, know when to step in, and when to let others take the lead. They provide the tools needed to achieve goals and create win-win situations despite cultural differences. They also see greatness in others.

In summary, global leadership is a deliberate fusion of commitment, connection and communication, based on trust, integrity and respect. It requires a well-designed strategy to navigate cultural divides, foster meaningful connections and empower others. The Culture SPIN Method provides the tools and framework to become a confident and successful global leader by design.

By following the four-step approach—Vision, Blueprint, Assembly, and Crossing the Bridge—you can develop the cross-cultural competency skills needed to thrive in today's interconnected world with the Culture SPIN Method™. It's about building bridges, expanding your reach, and creating lasting relationships through meaningful connections. Your leadership journey begins with a clear vision and ends with a transformative impact on the global stage.

Dr. Kristina Wachter, founder and CEO of Cross-Culture Connections, is a cross-cultural strategist and an award-winning business professor. She developed the Culture SPIN Method by working with leaders in business, travel, and cross-cultural communications from every continent—at all levels. She has years of academic and site-based research experience and taught cultural competency in major cities worldwide. Working in the corporate private sector as well as in small business ownership has given her further edge. Dr. Wachter has also authored textbooks, articles, and conducted cross-cultural case studies. To book her as a keynote speaker or for corporate cultural training, please reach out to her at:

Email: kristina@crosscultureconnections.com
Website: https://www.crosscultureconnections.com
LinkedIn: https://www.linkedin.com/in/kristina-gibby-wachter-phd-44659b64

CHAPTER NINE

Leading With Financial Wisdom: A Personal Journey
By Laura Davis

As I write this chapter, I want you to know that I am not just another financial planner with a business card. What I bring to the table is a journey through the complex world of finance, peppered with personal experiences and a deep understanding of what money really means to people. I'm not your typical financial advisor clad in a power suit, spouting off stock market jargon. I'm here to talk about something far more personal and, in many ways, more challenging—the psychology of money.

Money Scripts: The Hidden Forces

My fascination with finance isn't just about numbers and charts. It's about understanding why we think about money the way we do. Financial psychologists Bradley Klontz and Sonya Britt introduced a concept that resonated deeply with me—money scripts. These are the subconscious beliefs we all have about money, which shape our financial decisions and our lives.

Let me walk you through these scripts. Perhaps you'll see a bit of yourself in them, just like I did.

> **Money Avoidance:** This script is for those who view money negatively, believing that rich people are unethical or that they themselves don't deserve wealth. It's a tricky mindset that often sabotages financial success.

> **Money Worship:** Here, money is seen as the solution to all problems, a source of happiness and power. But this script can lead

to an endless chase for wealth, often at the expense of true contentment.

Money Vigilance: This one's close to my heart. It's about prudence, saving and treating money matters privately. It's a healthy script but can sometimes lead to excessive frugality or financial stress.

Money Status: For some, money is a symbol of status. It's about owning the latest and the best, using wealth as a measure of self-worth. But this can lead to dangerous financial decisions, driven by a desire to impress.

Take a moment to reflect on these scripts. Which one resonates with you? Understanding this can be a powerful first step in mastering your financial journey.

My Story: The Financial Crisis as a Turning Point

My personal story intertwines with a critical moment in our financial history—the 2008/2009 financial crisis. Fresh out of college, newly married and working in real estate in Atlanta, I witnessed first-hand the devastation caused by irresponsible financial practices. I sold foreclosed homes, seeing the real-life impact of a system that preyed on the vulnerable.

This experience was more than just a job; it was a lesson in the importance of financial literacy and integrity. It shaped my approach to financial advising, emphasizing not just the technicalities of money management but the human side of finance.

The Core Problem: The Overwhelming Nature of Money

In my years as a financial advisor, I've come to realize that most people are seeking one thing—reassurance that they'll be okay. The world of finance can be overwhelming, leading many to avoid confronting their financial realities. But avoidance only leads to more anxiety and uncertainty.

Money, in my view, should be a tool, not a tyrant. It should support your life, not control it. Helping clients reach this realization—to see money as an enabler, not an inhibitor—has been one of the most rewarding aspects of my career.

A Tale of Two Backgrounds: Shaping Financial Perspectives

Our attitudes toward money are often rooted in our upbringing. I come from an upper-middle-class family, while my husband grew up in a lower-middle-class household with a single mother. These contrasting backgrounds have influenced our relationship with money and with each other. Our journey together has been a lesson in understanding and respecting different financial perspectives, a crucial skill in both personal and professional life.

The Power of Money Scripts in Relationships

Understanding your own money script is not just vital for personal financial health, it's also crucial in relationships. I've seen clients struggle with financial conflicts rooted in differing money scripts. Recognizing and respecting these differences can be transformative, not just for financial planning but for the relationship as a whole.

The Three Pillars of Financial Comfort

In my pursuit to help people find clarity and comfort around money, I emphasize three key principles:

Know Your Values: What does "enough" look like for you? Understanding your values and what you truly need is crucial to achieving financial contentment.

Save for Your Lifestyle: It's essential to save enough during your working years to support your desired lifestyle in retirement. This requires a clear understanding of your current and future financial needs.

Manage Your Taxes: Taxes are a significant expense and managing them effectively can save you a considerable amount in the long run. This often-overlooked aspect of financial planning is critical for maximizing your resources.

The Journey to Financial Leadership

My path to becoming a financial advisor was not a straight line. It involved soul-searching, confronting personal and family financial challenges and a deep desire to make a meaningful impact in others' lives. This journey has imbued me with a sense of purpose and a passion for helping others navigate the complex world of finance.

Embracing Financial Leadership: A Deeper Dive

Financial leadership is more than just managing money, it's about guiding others through the labyrinth of financial decision-making, a journey often fraught with emotional and psychological hurdles. This journey, both personal and professional, has taught me invaluable lessons about the impact of financial well-being on all aspects of life.

The Interplay of Money and Emotions

One of the most significant insights from my career is the intricate link between money and emotions. Money isn't just currency, it's laden with emotional weight. It can symbolize security, power, love, or freedom. Recognizing this emotional dimension is crucial in understanding one's financial behaviors and, by extension, in guiding others towards healthier financial practices.

Financial Empathy: The Heart of Advising

As a financial advisor, empathy is my most powerful tool. Understanding clients' fears, dreams and challenges allows me to provide advice that resonates on a personal level. This empathetic approach transforms the advisor-client relationship from a mere business transaction into a journey of mutual trust and understanding.

The Reality of Financial Anxiety

Financial anxiety is a common thread among many of my clients. It's not just about the numbers in their bank accounts, it's about what those numbers represent—security, stability and sometimes self-worth. Addressing this anxiety requires a delicate balance of practical financial planning and psychological support, helping clients to navigate not only their finances but also their fears and beliefs about money.

The Role of Financial Education

I firmly believe that financial literacy is a key component of empowerment. My mission goes beyond advising; it's about educating. By demystifying financial concepts and making them accessible, I aim to empower clients to make informed decisions, fostering a sense of control and competence in their financial lives.

Overcoming Financial Obstacles: A Personal Tale

My own journey hasn't been without its financial obstacles. Early in my career, I faced challenges that tested my resilience and forced me to reevaluate my own money scripts. These experiences were pivotal, not just in shaping my financial outlook but in deepening my understanding of the struggles that many face in managing their finances.

Money Scripts in Action: Real-Life Examples

Let's delve into some real-life scenarios where money scripts played a crucial role. I've worked with clients who, under the influence of a Money Worship script, pursued wealth to the detriment of their personal relationships and happiness. Others, guided by Money Avoidance, shied away from financial opportunities, hindering their growth. These stories highlight the profound impact of our subconscious beliefs on our financial choices.

Financial Planning: More Than Numbers

In my practice, financial planning goes beyond spreadsheets and projections. It's about aligning financial strategies with personal values and goals. It's about creating a plan that not only makes sense on paper but feels right to the client. This holistic approach ensures that financial plans are not just effective but also personally meaningful.

Navigating Life's Financial Stages

Life is a series of financial stages, each with its unique challenges and opportunities. From starting a career to planning for retirement, each stage requires a different financial strategy. My role as an advisor is to guide clients through these stages, providing the tools and knowledge they need to navigate each phase successfully.

Building a Legacy of Financial Wisdom

One of my greatest aspirations is to leave a legacy of financial wisdom. By educating and empowering others, I hope to create a ripple effect, where the principles of sound financial management are passed down through generations, leading to a future where financial wellness is the norm, not the exception.

Conclusion: A Journey of Financial Transformation

Understanding your money script is just the beginning. The journey to financial wellness involves a deep dive into your values, goals and attitudes towards money. It's a journey that can bring peace of mind, clarity, and, ultimately, a sense of control over your financial destiny.

As I reflect on my journey, I realize that the true essence of financial leadership is the ability to transform lives. It's about turning financial anxiety into confidence, confusion into clarity, and dreams into realities.

It's a journey that I am honored to be a part of, and one that I will continue to pursue with passion and dedication.

If you're looking for more guidance, my book, *Earn Save Spend*, offers a comprehensive look at personal finance, tailored to provide you with the knowledge and tools you need to take charge of your financial future. Remember, the path to financial leadership is personal, and it starts with understanding yourself.

As a financial advisor for almost a decade, Laura Davis, CFP® has been helping people overcome their money blocks so they can spend their energy doing what they love. Laura's new illustrated personal finance book, Earn Save Spend, is accessible to everyone, whether they're just starting out or miles down their path to financial wellness. Whether it's one-on-one in her advisory practice or consulting with teams, Laura teaches people to transform their financial lives. To contact Laura, please reach out to her at:

Email: laura@financiallab.us
Website: www.financiallab.us
LinkedIn: https://www.linkedin.com/in/lauradmoney

CHAPTER TEN

The Power of Visionary Leadership
By Mia Reed

As a founder and chief executive officer of multiple organizations, I have always believed in the power of visionary leadership to bring about positive change in the world. As I reflect on my leadership journey, I am reminded of the life-changing moment when I first heard about horses being sent to slaughter, including pregnant ones. It was a shocking revelation that shook me to my core. While many people may have brushed it off as "not their problem," I decided to take ownership and create a solution. The horses I encountered were in a state of despair, physically and emotionally scarred by their past experiences. Their stories were heart-wrenching, and I knew that their lives depended on the love and care they would receive from us.

In a world where people often complain about issues and turn a blind eye, a true leader must step up and address problems. Taking ownership means recognizing that a problem has become your responsibility. It is about understanding that we all have the power to make a difference, no matter how big or small.

When I discovered that horses were facing such a terrible fate, I knew I had to take action. Within a few days, I had added a horse rescue to my ranch. We rescued four horses at a time, trailerful after trailerful. Each horse was terrified and we could see that in their eyes. We created a therapeutic relationship between children who have gone through traumatic challenges and horses who have also been mistreated. It became such a beautiful healing relationship between children and horses who needed each other.

I remember the day I first met Emily, a bright-eyed little girl with a heart full of dreams. She had always longed to be with horses and was excited at the very thought of even touching a horse for the first time.

On Emily's first day at my ranch, her eyes widened at the sight of the horses. As we walked through the pasture gate, the air was filled with the sweet scent of hay and the soft sounds of hooves on the ground. It was a place where dreams came true for both horses and children.

Her face lit up with joy and I could see the anticipation building within her. But there was one horse in particular that caught her attention: Starlight.

Starlight was a magnificent black horse with a white star on her forehead. She had been one of my first rescue horses, saved from a life of abuse and neglect. She had endured unimaginable pain and suffering, and her spirit had been broken. But despite her past, there was a glimmer of hope in her eyes.

As Emily approached Starlight, a sense of connection seemed to spark between them. Usually reserved and cautious, Starlight took a step closer to Emily, as if drawn to her kind and gentle nature. Emily reached out her hand, trembling with excitement, and gently touched Starlight's velvety nose. It was a moment of pure magic.

From that day forward, Emily and Starlight became inseparable. They spent hours together, grooming, playing and learning to trust one another. Emily's love and care began to heal the wounds that Starlight carried deep within her. And in return, Starlight taught Emily the true meaning of resilience and strength.

As the days turned into weeks, their bond grew stronger. Emily would whisper her dreams to Starlight, and the horse would listen intently, as if understanding every word. Together, they embarked on a journey of healing and transformation.

With each passing day, Starlight's spirit soared higher, and Emily's confidence blossomed.

Their story became an inspiration to all who witnessed it. The little girl and the rescued horse, both broken in their ways, had found solace and strength in each other's presence. They had shown the world that love and compassion could heal even the deepest wounds.

And so Emily's dream of being with horses had come true, but it was so much more than she had ever imagined. She had found not only a companion in Starlight but a lifelong friend who had taught her the power of love, resilience and the beauty of second chances.

This experience taught me the power of leading with strength and vision and the miracles that can happen. Instead of complaining or walking away, a leader should embrace challenges and actively seek ways to find solutions. More responsibility brings with it more challenges. Just a few of those challenges that came with rescuing horses included the logistics of feeding and caring for many horses, vet bills, building different horse pastures and barns, creating a complete horse program from scratch for foster children, and much more. We'd never had foals at the ranch but we pulled together and prepared for our new babies. When I met each one, I was filled with love. It was all worth it. I couldn't have had the confidence to take action without the right mindset and work ethic.

But how can one develop the mindset and skills to tackle problems head-on and provide strong leadership to effect change?

Allow me to introduce the "Elevate and Empower Technique." This unique personal development tool takes leadership training to a new level. It goes beyond surface-level affirmations and incorporates self-reflection, action steps and visualization to create lasting change and achieve meaningful results.

Step 1: Reflect and Reset

In this initial step, take a moment to pause and reflect on your current state of mind. Acknowledge any negative thoughts or limiting beliefs that may be holding you back. By bringing them into your awareness, you can gain clarity on the areas that need improvement. To begin the reset, mentally release these thoughts and let go of their power over you. This step sets the stage for a positive mindset shift.

Step 2: Affirmation Activation

Affirmations play a pivotal role in rewiring the subconscious mind and shifting beliefs. In this step, choose affirmations that align with your desired outcomes and resonate with your authentic self. These affirmations should be positive, present-tense statements that reflect the qualities and mindset you want to embody. Repeat these affirmations regularly to reinforce positive beliefs and reprogram your subconscious. To amplify their impact, visualize yourself already embodying these qualities and feel the associated positive emotions.

Step 3: Action Steps

Taking action is crucial for personal growth and achieving results. In this step, identify one or two small, manageable action steps that you can take immediately to move closer to your goals. Ensure these steps are meaningful and align with your desired outcomes. By breaking down your goals into actionable steps, you create a clear pathway to success. Commit to taking action today, which actively propels you towards your goals and builds momentum.

Step 4: Visualization and Future Pacing

Visualization is a powerful technique that helps create a mental image of your desired reality. Close your eyes and visualize yourself completing your action steps and achieving your goals. Engage all your senses to immerse yourself in this visualization, creating a vivid and compelling experience. This process enables you to overcome obstacles, feel confident and celebrate your achievements in advance. Mentally stepping into this successful version of yourself, known as future pacing, helps you embody the qualities and mindset associated with your accomplishments.

Step 5: Gratitude and Celebration

Gratitude is a transformative practice that shifts your focus to the positive aspects of life. Express gratitude for the progress you have made and the opportunities that lie ahead. Celebrate even the smallest victories and acknowledge your growth. Reinforce a positive mindset and boost your motivation. Take a moment to appreciate yourself for investing in personal development and cultivating self-love and self-compassion. Embrace a sense of gratitude and joy for the journey you are on and it will create a positive and empowering mindset.

By practicing the Elevate and Empower Technique daily, you dedicate a few minutes to intentionally align your mindset, take action and visualize your desired outcomes. This process transcends surface-level affirmations, incorporating self-reflection and gratitude to create a holistic approach to personal development. With consistent practice, this technique empowers you to overcome challenges, step into your full potential and achieve meaningful results in all aspects of life.

Transformation through the Elevate and Empower Technique

Allow me to share my personal story of how the Elevate and Empower Technique transformed not only me as a leader but also my company. As a CEO of several organizations, I faced numerous challenges and decisions daily. I was often asked how I was able to lead with such confidence and authority while maintaining a sense of peace, staying focused not on problems but on being the solution. I created the Elevate and Empower Technique, a professional and personal development tool that moved myself and my clients forward as visionary resilient leaders.

Through deep reflection (Step 1), I identified the limiting beliefs that were hindering my progress. I released them, allowing a positive mindset shift. Next, I chose powerful affirmations (Step 2) that aligned with my vision for myself and my company. By consistently repeating these affirmations and immersing myself in visualizations (Step 4), I reprogrammed my mind, leading to increased confidence and resilience.

Taking meaningful action steps (Step 3) allowed me to tackle issues at their core, cultivating a problem-solving mindset. I broke down complex problems into manageable steps and committed to making progress each day. This proactive approach transformed how I led my team and addressed challenges.

The gratitude and celebration (Step 5) component played a vital role in maintaining momentum and fostering a positive work culture. By expressing gratitude and celebrating victories, big and small, we created an environment of appreciation and motivation. This shift brought our team closer together and elevated our collective performance.

The Elevate and Empower Technique, with its holistic approach, has not only transformed my leadership style but also significantly impacted my company. Through problem-solving and ownership, coupled with this unique personal development tool, I have been able to solve complex issues and inspire my team to do the same.

In conclusion, leadership development requires taking ownership and embracing problem-solving. True leaders don't shy away from problems; they step up and say, "It's my problem now." The Elevate and Empower Technique provides a structured and transformative process to develop excellent leadership skills. By reflecting, affirming, taking action, visualizing, and expressing gratitude, individuals can achieve personal growth, overcome challenges, and unlock their full potential as leaders.

Throughout this chapter, we have explored the concept of taking ownership as a leader and the importance of actively seeking solutions. We discussed the consequences of the "not my problem" mentality and the need for leaders to step up and address issues. We introduced the Elevate and Empower Technique, a unique process that combines self-reflection, action steps, and visualization to create lasting change and achieve meaningful results.

By adopting an ownership mindset, leaders inspire and motivate others to do the same. They create a culture of problem-solving and continuous improvement within their organizations. Through the Elevate and Empower Technique, leaders can develop the necessary skills and mindset to tackle challenges head-on, empower their team members, and create innovative solutions.

It is important to remember that leadership is not just about solving problems; it is also about creating a vision, inspiring others, and fostering a positive work culture. By taking ownership and actively seeking solutions, leaders set an example for their team members and create an environment where everyone feels empowered to contribute their ideas and expertise.

In conclusion, leadership development is a lifelong journey that requires continuous learning and growth. By embracing the mindset of ownership and utilizing tools like the Elevate and Empower Technique, leaders can navigate challenges with confidence, inspire their teams, and create a positive impact in their organizations and communities. So, let us all strive to be leaders who take ownership, solve problems, and create a better future for ourselves and those around us.

Mia is a highly sought-after keynote speaker, author, CEO and expert in executive leadership driven by the burning questions that many have asked her, "How do you do it all, impact the world, and still love your life?" Through interactive workshops, retreats and powerful coaching, Mia empowers leaders to develop the high-performance skills and mindset necessary to drive personal and professional success. With her inspiring speaking style, Mia embodies thought leadership and presence. She is the ideal choice for your next event as her ability to connect with audiences and deliver actionable insights will leave a lasting impact, inspiring attendees to reach new heights in their leadership journey and create a life they truly love.

To book Mia as a speaker, workshop facilitator, or coach, contact her at:
Website: www.leaderwithvision.com
Email: booking@leaderwithvision.com

CHAPTER ELEVEN

The Power of Leading Yourself First
By Samantha Taylor

In my life and business, I have discovered that it is often more difficult to lead yourself than others. Ironically, the better you become at leading yourself, the more effective you become at leading others.

Although I was technically leading others in my career as a fitness and weight loss coach, I was failing to lead myself by not taking adequate care of my health. It took me a while to realize that this disconnect was affecting my leadership abilities.

I was making poor food choices that were impacting my mental clarity, mood, ability to handle stress and making me gain weight. And I was starting to have health issues pile up such as prediabetes and skin cancer. At the time I was only in my late 30's but I was already experiencing massive memory and cognition issues. This started to concern me because both of my grandmothers died with Alzheimer's, and they were both big sugar eaters like I was.

As a personal trainer who was leading others down the path of making healthier choices and getting into the best shape of their lives, I battled with my personal health issues in isolation. As I continued to help my clients have amazing results, I felt like a fraud because I knew what I struggled with behind closed doors: I was a food addict who was addicted to sugar and a compulsive binge eater. I was living from food-craving to food-craving and turning to food for comfort. This was robbing me of my mental focus and energy while stealing my happiness, brain power and integrity.

The secrecy around my unhealthy lifestyle and relationship with food engulfed me in shame but I didn't know how to change it, despite all the book knowledge I had about eating healthy. I could inspire others to transform their lives, but I couldn't get myself to do it.

Leaders are expected to coach, guide and inspire others, yet I wasn't doing that for myself. I was out of control in SO many areas of my life. I lacked self-discipline and was not walking in integrity as I would frequently break promises to myself despite "trying to do better." This left me feeling like an imposter.

Victory with my food issues really started when I got "busted" in the middle of one of my overeating fests at a pizza buffet. I snuck in there, hoping nobody would recognize me, which was not easy to do since I was a local celebrity writing articles in the paper, had a radio show and had a TV spot on the news!

After I had gorged at the buffet on over five thousand calories, the server looked at me, then looked at the empty plates she was picking up and asked, "Aren't you that health expert in the paper?" Ohhh, ouch, busted!

"Oh this?" I responded. "This is a cheat meal. You didn't read that article?"

She replied something like, "Whatever," and walked away.

My heart sank because I knew this wasn't just a cheat meal; I was cheating in my whole life, and I just got called out for it. Although that embarrassing moment was painful, it was a gift because it made me face who I had become and what a lie I was living. As I drove back to the gym to train my next clients, I was in tears, questioning my career and if I should just quit because I felt like such a fraud.

I got to the gym and hopped on the treadmill to burn off some of the calories, the same treadmill that I had put hundreds of clients on. Tears were streaming down my face. I felt absolutely hopeless and didn't know how I was ever going to overcome these struggles with food. As I was praying, I had a strong awareness of my body as a gift from God and that I was abusing my body with the choices I was making. But honestly, I felt trapped. I didn't know how to change, which sounds ironic since I was "the expert" others looked up to! Shouldn't I of all people be able to figure this out?!

I remembered hearing a saying that "out of the heart, flow the issues of life" so I thought about taking ownership of the poor choices I was making. I needed to move beyond head knowledge and have a heart change and start to look at why I was making the choices I was. I realized I needed to start treating my body with more respect as the gift that it was, that I needed to have a different relationship with food.

I knew I had to face the truth and admit to myself that I was using food for comfort, stress eating and choosing food for just flavor and convenience, instead of for fuel.

Until that moment, I hadn't fully grasped the impact of my food choices on handling my stress level, confidence and overall happiness. It dawned on me that adopting a whole approach encompassing my mind, body and spirit was essential, and that the habits I had in my life were something I could change. I felt a new surge of hope when I left that treadmill, but I knew I had some work to do.

After I had left the corporate gym to go off on my own, I quickly found it was a different level of skills required to own a business than be an employee. I went from being the #1 trainer out of 2,000 trainers, to having a hard time growing my business. It didn't help that my brain always seemed foggy, and I just couldn't focus. I knew my addiction to sugar was a part of this. My late husband of 29 years who was my personal trainer said to me, "I bet if you got off sugar, your business would explode because you would think more clearly—and you will also be walking in integrity with what you teach."

Even though that hurt to hear, I knew the amount of sugar I was eating, and it was causing me a lot of issues. It was time to go to the next level and take up his challenge. I gave a gift to myself for my 40th birthday and resolved to go 90 days with no sugar. What I found was shocking! I couldn't believe that my cravings for sugar were completely gone! And I felt like I was on some super power supplement for my brain when I got the sugar out of my body.

Over the next four years, my ability to focus was so impacted that I was able to go from being a struggling business owner to someone who opened five personal training studios with 38 employees and built a seven-figure business! I walked in a different level of authority and confidence and my leadership abilities skyrocketed. There is no way that would have happened had I not stepped up and led myself in taking care of my own health first. Prioritizing my physical well-being stands out as the single most impactful decision I've ever made in my life and business. Sadly, most people don't realize the positive and negative correlation between their physical health and how it impacts every area of their life and career or business.

One major issue in America is that the population is now 70% overweight and half of that number is considered obese. Roughly two out of three U.S. adults are overweight and one out of those three are obese. One big reason is we have filled our lives with habits of convenience and are eating foods that contribute to this problem. Another reason is most people were not taught to make health a priority, so they really don't know the true cost of what they are doing to themselves.

Studies show that about 95% of those who lose a large amount of weight normally gain it back and more. Those statistics are quite discouraging unless you turn your focus to the 5% that do keep it off. What are they doing differently? And how can you learn from them and do the same thing?

I have learned some of the answers to these questions from my own struggles and victories but also in my personal training career, where I have helped over 10,000 clients lose weight, as well as thousands more in my online programs.

Did you know that scientific research shows that certain foods can trigger parts in the brain that mimic the same areas that are stimulated with drugs? And that these foods can cause you to lose the ability for self-control from the effect they have on the chemicals in your brain?

When it comes to thinking clearly at your job or working on a project, even a single episode of high blood sugar from food choices can impact the brain, leading to impairments in cognitive function, memory and attention. Sugar highs and lows in our blood sugar can contribute to symptoms such as brain fog, sluggishness, exhaustion, depression and anxiety. I found that these effects would happen for me not only from what I ate but also if I overate in a meal, which was often.

When it comes to weight loss, it's not just about a number on a scale because everyone's body is different. It's about the health of the body and the number of medical issues we expose ourselves to when we regularly consume foods that contribute to excess body fat. Losing body fat is a side benefit to getting healthy and taking care of your body.

A lot of weight loss programs overcomplicate things and don't help people make incremental adjustments. To have lasting victory with my eating, I had to work on it in stages and what took me 10 years to figure out, I now show people in months.

The mind can only handle so much change at once and that is one of the biggest issues people have with succeeding at most weight loss programs. They read a book that has a list of 75 things to change and get all fired up and proclaim, "I am going to do this!" You try but quickly find out that you can't possibly make that many changes overnight. Then you resort back to your old, familiar habits. This is the perpetual cycle so many are on. It's like trying to climb out of a pit up a ladder by getting to the top in one giant leap, instead of going one rung at a time. We're not superheroes and we don't live in a fairy tale land. You can't just snap your fingers and all the sudden "POOF," everything is fixed. That's just not how it works.

Until we have a different relationship with food, our experience is not going to change. And by relationship, I mean how you interact with food. Do you have a dysfunctional relationship with food where you experience some temporary pleasure but it's ultimately abusive and unhealthy? Do your food choices support the results you want in health or a certain weight loss goal you may have? Do they support keeping your brain sharp so you can focus on your job or business?

Many programs talk about dieting to lose weight but few talk about habits, emotional eating or a dysfunctional relationship with food. The food we eat and the habits that we have are things that we've done for years and are ingrained patterns of behavior.

When we do an action repeatedly, something develops in our brain called a neural pathway that makes that behavior easier and more automatic—that's what a habit is. It's really the brain's way of protecting you because its goal is to make processes automatic to conserve energy. Unfortunately, the brain is indifferent to whether something is a positive or a negative habit. So, if you get "triggered" when you see brownies and are tempted, you go into autopilot and your brain knows exactly what to do with those brownies! Eat them! Why? Because that is what your brain has been conditioned to do. And if you are like I was, I would have more than one!

Taking leadership of yourself is the same principle as leading a team. It's somebody who has the courage to step up and recognize when something is not working and takes charge of fixing it. This is why I give my clients practical tools to help them replace old habits with more beneficial ones.

A tool to help you step up and be the leader of your health and wellness is to apply these three simple steps:

1. Realize where you are and OWN it by taking responsibility that YOU are the manager of your body. You are the only one who can decide to take care of it, and it starts with being honest with yourself about where you are, as difficult as that may be.

   One way you can see how your habits are impacting you is to take a minute to really think about the road you have been on with your health and ask yourself these questions: How are you REALLY doing? How do you feel when you wake up? How do you feel physically? How's your blood work? What has your doctor said to you about your health? What is it costing you now in your life? And how is your energy level, happiness or productivity?

2. Think about the primary thing you do that causes your biggest issue with something like weight gain or food cravings. We all know what our main issues are if we stop and take the time to think about it. Once you have an answer, I want you to immediately grab a pen and write down one SMALL step you can take to help you improve in that area. Then once you apply that small change a few times and you realize it's not that difficult, then repeat the process. Think of one MORE small thing you can do to improve in that same area. Then little by little, rung by rung, you will climb out of that pit of frustration and improve greatly because you have built confidence that you can make a change in your life.

3. You must track your progress because you cannot expect what you don't inspect. By writing down the improvement you said you were going to make, reminding yourself to do it AND tracking it to make sure you ARE doing it, that helps you to focus and stick to what you said you were going to do.

If you apply these three steps, you will see an impact, but YOU must DO them. They aren't going to just happen without you focusing on them. Most things worth having in life are going to take some effort but you will reap the benefits! Plus, when you begin to lead yourself down this critical path of improving self-care, you will be a better leader to those around you because the best leaders lead by example.

EVERYTHING that we do comes from our body. Think about it ... without your body, you have no life on earth! So, I encourage you to have a new appreciation for your body as the most valuable asset that you have. If you don't take care of it, you will regret it. If you do, you will reap the benefits.

Invest some time to dig deep to find out WHY you have adopted the habits that you have in the first place. This will increase your likelihood of success. A trained specialist can help you improve your relationship with food, so it serves you instead of harming you. It's worth doing the work and self-discovery. It's powerful to ask yourself questions like, "Where are you going to be in the next 5 or 10 years if you don't take leadership of your body? Are you going to be happy with the outcome? Or are you going to wish you would have made some different choices?"

There is great freedom in realizing you can do something about taking control of your food choices because it gives you the power to do something instead of feeling helpless and thinking it's out of your control. God gave us a gift of this miraculous body to take care of and if you don't, you can't just trade it in when it falls apart … it's the only one you get!

Taking care of your health is the one thing you can't pay people to do for you. Nobody is going to show up and make you CHOOSE the food that you put on the fork that goes into your mouth. Don't let the wake-up call be a doctor telling you that you've got a disease that you possibly could have prevented.

You're not going to solve the problem that you are in with the same thinking that got you there because your thinking must be different to get different results. That's why you want to learn from someone who has already done it and is going to help you rethink how you are doing things. I have figured out many simple and highly effective ways for you to implement and start to see your life become the one you design instead of just accepting whatever happens to you. If you would like to go deeper in exploring how to have this victory, I put together a free course for you on how to do exactly that. Plus, I have a bonus video on how to use my "Fast Forward 5TM" method that helped me immediately make better food choices!

Go to this webpage to access your free course and start to experience the power of leading yourself first! www.SamanthaTaylor.com/leadyourself

Samantha Taylor, a highly experienced specialist with 32 years in the health and fitness industry, has successfully helped individuals shed 100

tons of fat through her Transformation Coaching, which encompasses the mind, body and spirit. Samantha intimately understands the challenges of yo-yo dieting. Her own journey began when she recognized the impact of her eating habits on her mental focus and productivity, prompting her to leave the corporate gym and establish five personal training studios. Through her dedication and expertise, she built a thriving seven-figure business and has trained over 10,000 clients. Samantha's accomplishments also include hosting her own radio and TV show on health. She specializes in coaching individuals who seek personal growth beyond conventional dieting advice, addressing emotional aspects and promoting mindful practices. Going beyond superficial dieting, Samantha's philosophy delves into the emotional and psychological ties to food, leading individuals towards a transformative lifestyle that transcends mere weight loss, fostering improved self-esteem, energy and overall well-being. Samantha shares her expertise as a keynote speaker, author and through various media platforms such as TV, radio and podcasts. Additionally, she offers online coaching programs to support her clients on their personal journeys.

If you would like to book Samantha to speak at your next event, visit: www.SamanthaTaylor.com/bookspeaking

Email: booksamantha@samanthataylor.com
Website: https://www.SamanthaTaylor.com
LinkedIn: https://www.linkedin.com/in/samanthataylor333

THANK YOU FOR YOUR REVIEW

Love this book? Don't forget to leave a review!

Every review matters, and it matters a *lot!*

Head over to Amazon or wherever you purchased this book to leave an

honest review for our book.

We thank you endlessly.

ABOUT DEFINING MOMENTS PRESS

Built for aspiring authors who are looking to share transformative ideas with others throughout the world, Defining Moments Press offers life coaches, healers, business professionals, and other non-fiction or self-help authors a comprehensive solution to getting their books published without breaking the bank or taking years. Defining Moments Press prides itself on bringing readers and authors together to find tools and solutions.

As an alternative to self-publishing or signing with a major publishing house, we offer full profits to our authors, low-priced author copies, and simple contract terms.

Most authors get stuck trying to navigate the technical end of publishing. The comprehensive publishing services offered by Defining Moments Press mean that your book will be designed by an experienced graphic artist, available in printed, hard copy format, and coded for all eBook readers, including the Kindle, iPad, Nook, and more.

We handle all the technical aspects of your book creation so you can spend more time focusing on your business that makes a difference for other people.

Defining Moments Press founder, publisher, and #1 bestselling author Melanie Warner has over 20 years of experience as a writer, publisher, master life coach, and accomplished entrepreneur.

You can learn more about Warner's innovative approach to self-publishing or take advantage of free training and education at: MyDefiningMoments.com.

DEFINING MOMENTS BOOK PUBLISHING

If you're like many authors, you have wanted to write a book for a long time, maybe you have even started a book ... but somehow, as hard as you have tried to make your book a priority, other things keep getting in the way.

Some authors have fears about their ability to write or whether anyone will value what they write or buy their book. For others, the challenge is making the time to write their book or having accountability to finish it.

It's not just finding the time and confidence to write that is an obstacle. Most authors get overwhelmed with the logistics of finding an editor, finding a support team, hiring an experienced designer, and figuring out all the technicalities of writing, publishing, marketing, and launching a book. Others have written a book and might have even published it but did not find a way to make it profitable.

For more information on how to participate in our next

Defining Moments Author Training program, visit

www.MyDefiningMoments.com

Or email

support@MyDefiningMoments.com

OTHER #1 BESTSELLING BOOKS BY
DEFINING MOMENTS ™ PRESS

Defining Moments: Coping With the Loss of a Child—Melanie Warner

Defining Moments SOS: Stories of Survival—Melanie Warner and Amber Torres

Write your Bestselling Book in 8 Weeks or Less and Make a Profit
—Even if No One Has Ever Heard of You—Melanie Warner

Become Brilliant: Roadmap From Fear to Courage—Shiran Cohen

Unspoken: Body Language and Human Behavior For Business—Shiran Cohen

Rise, Fight, Love, Repeat: Ignite Your Morning Fire—Jeff Wickersham

Life Mapping: Decoding the Blueprint of Your Soul—Karen Loenser

Ravens and Rainbows: A Mother-Daughter Story of Grit, Courage and Love After Death
*—L. Grey and Vanessa Lynn

Pivot You! 6 Powerful Steps to Thriving During Uncertain Times—Suzanne R. Sibilla

A Workforce Inspired: Tools to Manage Negativity and Support a Toxic-Free
Workplace—Dolores Neira

Journey of 1000 Miles: A Musher and His Huskies' Journey on the Century-Old Klondike
Trails—Hank DeBruin and Tanya McCready

7 Unstoppable Starting Powers: Powerful Strategies for Unparalleled Results From Your
First Year as a New Leader—Olusegun Eleboda

Bouncing Back From Divorce With Vitality & Purpose: A Strategy For Dads
*—Nigel J Smart, PHD

Focus on Jesus and Not the Storm: God's Non-negotiables to Christians in America
*—Keith Kelley

Stepping Out, Moving Forward: Songs and Devotions—Jacqueline O'Neil Kelley

Time Out for Time In: How Reconnecting With Yourself Can Help You Bond With Your Child in a Busy Word—Jerry Le

The Sacred Art of Off Mat Yoga: Whisper of Wisdom Forever—Shakti Barnhill

The Beauty of Change: The Fun Way for Women to Turn Pain Into Power & Purpose—Jean Amor Ramoran

From No Time to Free Time: 6 Steps to Work/Life Balance for Business Owners—Christoph Nauer

Self-Healing for Sexual Abuse Survivors: Tired of Just Surviving, Time to Thrive—Nickie V. Smith

Prepared Bible Study Lessons: Weekly Plans for Church Leaders—John W. Warner

Frog on a Lily Pad—Michael Lehre

How to Effectively Supercharge Your Career as a CEO—Giorgio Pasqualin

Rising From Unsustainable: Replacing Automobiles and Rockets—J.P. Sweeney

Food—Life's Gift for Healing: Simple, Delicious & Life Saving Whole Food Plant Based Solutions—Angel and Terry Grier

Harmonize All of You with All: The Leap Ahead in Self-Development—Artie Vipperla

Powerless to Powerful: How to Stop Living in Fear and Start Living Your Life—Kat Spencer

Living with Dirty Glasses: How to Clean those Dirty Glasses and Gain a Clearer Perspective of Your Life—Leah Montani

The Road Back to You: Finding Your Way After Losing a Child to Suicide—Trish Simonson

Gavin Gone: Turning Pain into Purpose to Create a Legacy—Rita Gladding

The Health Nexus: TMJ, Sleep Apnea, and Facial Development, Causations and Treatment—Robert Perkins DDS

Samantha Jean's Rainbow Dream: A Young Foster Girl's Adventure into the Colorful World of Fruits & Vegetables—AJ Autieri-Luciano

Live Your Truth: An Arab Man's Journey In Finding the Courage to Live His Truth As He Identifies as Gay and Coping with Mental Illness Paperback—David Rabadi

Unstoppable: A Parent's Survival Guide for Special Education Services with an IEP or 504 Plan—Raja B. Marhaba

Please, Excuse My Brave: Overcoming Fear and Living Out Your Purpose—Anisa Wesley

Drawing with Purpose: A Sketch Journal—Rick Alonzo

NY Coffee: Love Fulfilled in the Little Things—Craig Lieckfelt

Good Work: How Gen X and Millennials are the Dream Team for Doing Good When Collaborating—Erin-Kate Whitcomb

Rescue Me: Guided Self-Healing for First Responders: Conquering Depression, Anxiety, PTSD & Moral Injury—David Hogan

Treasures In Grief: Discover 7 Spiritual Gifts Hidden in Your Pain—Lo Anne Mayer

We Three: Their Beginnings—Derek Drummond

Made in the USA
Las Vegas, NV
12 March 2024

87069617R00069